How CARNFORTH Steamed into the 20th Century

By

MARION RUSSELL

Published by Lundarien Press, UK

ISBN 978-1-910816-69-1

For more info and other books in this series:

www.lundarienpress.com

OTHER BOOKS IN THE

A HISTORY OF CARNFORTH SERIES

1. How Carnforth Grew - a simple outline to 1900AD

3. A Childhood in Carnforth

CONTENTS

INTRODUCTION

As a continuation of my simple outline of *HOW CARNFORTH GREW*, this is an attempt to carry the story on from 1900 - 1914, as seen through the eyes of my mother ANNIE WILKINSON (nee Barnham) as she grew from girlhood, through her teens and her long courtship to my father TOM WILKINSON, until they eventually married in 1914.

Annie, the eldest of 6 children - Arthur, Willie, Ella, Frank, and Bertha - was the squirrel of the family, storing photographs, school books, samplers and also souvenir leaflets, pamphlets and newspaper cuttings appertaining to events held in Carnforth. How these were safely hidden from the prying eyes and interfering fingers of her young siblings I do not know! When my mother died, aged 86, in 1974, I had the heart rending task of breaking-up what had once been my home at 31 Haws Hill, and for her sake I felt I had to hold on to her keepsakes which she had treasured so long. They have proved to be my links to her (and Carnforth's) past, and it would have given her great satisfaction to know that.

As viewed from the Barnham angle, this look-back at the Carnforth of almost a century ago is not a story full of adventure and excitement. It is more than likely that others could tell far more interesting and thrilling tales about their ancestors who lived here, and were employed at the Iron Works, perhaps.

Getting just a small book printed and on sale is a slow and exhausting process for an old person like me. I felt it was all worthwhile however, when I was told, by word of mouth, letters and phone-calls, that "HOW CARNFORTH GREW" was being read, not only in many parts of Britain, but overseas in Australia, New Zealand, America, Canada, Austria etc. It gave me a nice warm feeling to think that, for a while, it was linking former Carnforthians together in thoughts about our hometown.

Even our famous Right Honourable Lord Cecil Parkinson of Carnforth was in the chain of thoughts, and wrote that he had read it with great interest, which heartened me. I'd held back on having it printed because I'd feared that most people would find it boring whilst others would be critical and on the lookout for errors.

Outsiders have said to me over the years that they rush through Carnforth because it looks such a grey, miserable place. I'd like them to see a letter I received recently from an octogenarian, a member of a well-known local family, who left our town when he was 8 years old. In it he wrote, "My heart is still in Carnforth!"

I have been made aware that there are many people who have fond memories of our hometown.

Good wishes to them all!

Marion Russell, Carnforth, 1998

INTO THE 20TH CENTURY

By the dawn of the new century, Carnforth had grown from a small hamlet with a population of only 290 in the year 1851, to a busy little Victorian town with 3,040 inhabitants.

The Industrial Revolution had changed Great Britain from an agricultural to an industrial country. Clever inventions had led to the building of large factories, mills and ironworks with coal-devouring blast furnaces. New methods had had to be found to move heavy, bulky good quickly and efficiently.

Resulting from these events, two factors had led to the rapid growth of Carnforth's population. The first occurred when people had been brought from the Midlands (especially from Dudley) to work here in the Haematite Ironworks, established in 1864. The second was the arrival of families drawn from Cumberland, Yorkshire and Westmorland to work on the railway here.

Carnforth had become a busy junction on the Lancaster-Carlisle Main Line when the Furness Railway was opened in 1857, and later in 1866 when a line was built from Carnforth, through the 1,230 yards long tunnel at Melling, to Wennington on the Midland Railway Line which connects Leeds to Lancaster. Trains could then steam north, south, east and west from Carnforth.

A new breed of Carnforthian was born as all the

newcomers, with their various cultures and dialects, settled down here and learnt to live and work amicably together.

WELCOMING THE NEW CENTURY

In all probability, Carnforth people welcomed in the 20th Century by meeting on the Market Ground at the bottom of Market Street, opposite The Station Hotel. No market had been held there for many years, but as a piece of spare land it had become the centre for many outdoor activities in our town.

As the pointers of men's pocket watches reached the midnight hour, it is likely that all the railway engines in the marshalling yards would sound their whistles, and the assembled crowd would cheer, cross hands together and sing Auld Lang Syne. *[This was a New Year custom which lasted many years.]*

SOUVENIRS

To commemorate the 19th century and welcome in the 20th, two souvenirs could be bought at shops in Market Street. One costing 6d (40 for £1) was a copy of The Daily Mail newspaper printed throughout, words and pictures, in gleaming gold.

The other was a sheet of piano music - a march entitled 'Dawn of the Century'. On the cover was a picture of an ethereal maiden standing on tip-toe on a winged wheel surmounting the globe. In one hand she held aloft a standard, and a finger of her other hand was pressing a switch and flashing out streaks of ELECTRICITY. Surrounding her were pictures portraying the wonderful inventions of the 19th century: a sewing machine, telephone, dynamo, harvesting machine, a train, a tram and, last of all, a CAR.

Folk wondered what amazing inventions the 20th century would bring!

OUR EMPIRE

At the beginning of the 20th century, Great Britain had a powerful empire which spanned the world and was said to have one heart, one head, one language and one policy.

Carnforth had celebrated as joyous occasions the Golden and the Diamond Jubilees of our good Queen Victoria, who was now an old lady nearing the end of her reign.

Sadly our country was at war overseas. A stubborn breed of Dutch settlers (Boers) in South Africa had revolted against 'the just sovereignty of the British Queen'. It was optimistically prophesied that our soldiers would soon be victors in that BOER WAR.

TRANSPORT

Carnforth railwaymen had always found progress in transport a very interesting topic. Up till now, all the inventions concerned with the movement of people and goods had been on a terrestrial level.

Getting ready to make deliveries from the Railway Goods yard, entrance from Warton Road near the Iron Works.

A new dimension was added however when the men read in their newspapers that a German Count, Ferdinand von Zeppelin, had invented a huge airship. At its trials on Lake Geneva in July, it actually rose into the air and flew for the first time at the amazing height of 12 feet.

Lads in the Endowed School playground enjoyed chuffing about as railway engines. Trying to fly around as airships was going to present problems, as young Willie Barnham pointed out to his pals! *[Those wonderful Zeppelins were to become very bad news for Great Britain just over a decade later.]*

A LAUNCHING

On November 9th, 1900, some of our adventurous townspeople journeyed by train to BARROW-IN-FURNESS across Morecambe Bay. They were heading for VICKERS SHIP-YARDS to witness a wonderful event: the launching of the LARGEST and most POWERFUL warship in all the world. Crowds cheered as it slid down the slipway.

Sadly it was flying the Rising Sun flag of Japan, not the UNION JACK!

THE BOER WAR

Towards the end of the year news from the war zone in South Africa was bad. 11,000 of our troops had died: 4,000 in battle and 7,000 killed by diseases such as dysentery and enteric fever.

As far as is known, no Carnforth men fought in the Boer War, but its battles were fought in street games: up Highfield Terrace way and down Grovvner (Grosvenor Place) "THE GOODIES" (Lord Roberts and the brave British troops) attacked "THE BADDIES" (Kruger and his fierce Boers.)

[As history unrolled, street enemies changed: Cops v Robbers, Cowboys v Indians, Britons v Germans etc.]

1901

The Mannex Directory of Lancaster, Morecambe and District stated:

"CARNFORTH is a flourishing and progressive town. It is an important POST OFFICE CENTRE at the JUNCTION of the L.N.W. and MIDLAND RAILWAYS, and the terminus of the FURNESS LINE".

DEATH OF QUEEN VICTORIA

On Jan 22nd, Carnforth mourned with the rest of Britain at the sad news of the old Queen's death. She had reigned for 63 GLORIOUS YEARS and was the head of Britain's far-flung empire on which the sun never set.

Saturday February 2nd was the day of her funeral. A form of United Prayer and Praise was held simultaneously at our Parish Church, the Emmanuel Congregational Church and the Wesleyan Chapel. Memorial leaflets, printed in Carnforth by the Visitor Company, were given to each worshipper (my mother kept hers all her life).

After singing the hymn "NOW THE LABOURER'S TASK IS OE'R," the congregations left the churches and made their way to the Market Ground. There, the town's Brass Band led everyone in the singing of the National Anthem.

Our Royal Family warmly welcomed Kaiser

Wilhelm II of Germany to the Queen's funeral. A few weeks before, he had been made a Field Marshall in the British Army by our new sovereign King Edward VII, who was his uncle.

[This German ruler was to become our deadly enemy ere many years were past!]

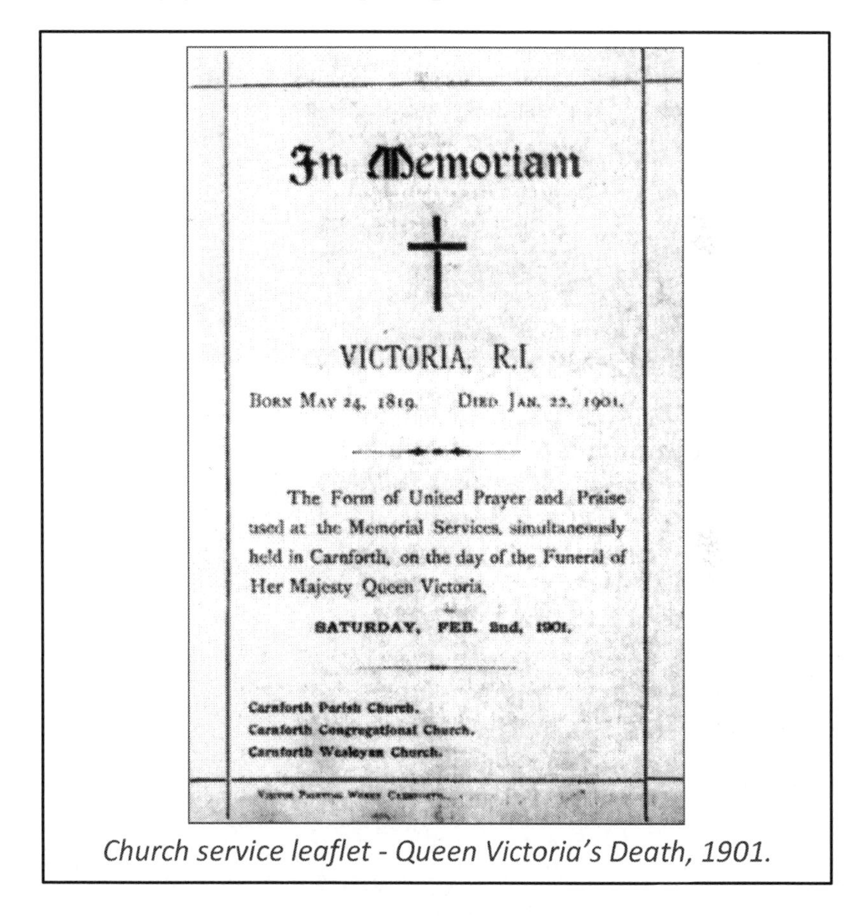

In Memoriam

VICTORIA, R.I.

Born May 24, 1819. Died Jan. 22, 1901.

The Form of United Prayer and Praise used at the Memorial Services, simultaneously held in Carnforth, on the day of the Funeral of Her Majesty Queen Victoria.

SATURDAY, FEB. 2nd, 1901.

Carnforth Parish Church.
Carnforth Congregational Church.
Carnforth Wesleyan Church.

Church service leaflet - Queen Victoria's Death, 1901.

PLANTING FAMILY ROOTS

In the census of 1901, Carnforth's population was recorded as 3,040, showing an amazing ten-fold increase over the last 50 years.

Among the many people who had come to live here in search of good work was RICHARD WILKINSON (my paternal grandfather, born in 1856). He had been registered in 1881 as a railway labourer, age 24, living in lodgings at 4 Stanley Street.

One of a family of 10 children, he had left his home in Cabus (Scorton) and gone into farm service before he was 13 years old. Perhaps seeing wonderful trains steam through his village had inspired him to escape from a life of possible 'slavery' on a farm and to seek his fortune on one of Carnforth's railways.

Richard married Isabelle Jackson, who was brought up on a farm in Yealand Redmayne, and he eventually became a GOODS GUARD. The family lived in THE DOLLY-TUB ROW, Cragbank, then in HOPE TERRACE (Cragbank Road) and finally at 38 Grosvenor Place, which had been built especially for railway employees to rent. Their 2 sons, John and THOMAS (my father) both went to work at the L.N.W.R. sheds on leaving school.

[John emigrated to Canada, but my father slowly climbed the ladder of promotion: knocker-up, locomotive cleaner, footplate fireman, and eventually DRIVER. Carnforth people of today might find it interesting to go to Lancaster Reference Library and look-up their FAMILY TREES to discover what originally brought their ancestors to live here.]

A FIRST AIDER

It was the railways that had also brought my maternal grandparents, WILLIAM and MARY BARNHAM, to live here around 1893. They had bought number 39 in the newly-built second block of houses at the top of Highfield Terrace. The price had been about £90, which was most probably borrowed from the Carnforth Co-operative Society's Cottage Fund, and repaid weekly in the form of rent.

William, a railwayman, had worked at Leeds, Shipley and Eldroth before being appointed as signalman at the Midland Line's East-Junction box here.

In April, aged 38 and father of 6 children, he received a certificate signed by our Dr Jackson (surgeon instructor) for attending a course at the Carnforth Branch of the St John's Ambulance Brigade.

At this time, our town had 2 Station Managers. Mr W Farnworth was in charge of the London-North-Western Railway line, and Mr Thomas Peel was station master for the Midland Line, which had an entrance from Warton Road.

The Goods Agent was Mr R Unsworth.

THE VICAR

Rev Scott, M.A., the second vicar of the Parish Church, moved into the new vicarage built up

North Road. The house stood alone, and had beautiful panoramic views over the canal below to KELLET SEEDS (a wooded hill) and to the lovely mountains of the Pennine Chain.

[Welmar Estate now covers the hillside near that old Vicarage.]

EDUCATION

The NATIONAL SCHOOL (formerly called The Endowed School) at the junction of Lancaster Road with Haws Hill, and the BRITISH SCHOOL (off Hawk Street near the Congregational Church) had headmasters named respectively Mr DAN MILLER and Mr R T BARNARD. Both were very strict disciplinarians (and are still remembered today!)

Mr Miller lived at PLANE TREE HOUSE in Lower North Road, and he was such a renowned citizen that the road's name was changed to Miller's Lane. *[The rise up to the Kellet Road junction from his home is still called MILLER'S HILL by all true Carnforthians].*

Another well-known member of the community who gave his name to an area of our town was the Rev J A FIDDLER. He had been Carnforth's first vicar c.1869-1897, and had conducted services in the Lecture Room over the Endowed School before CHRIST CHURCH was built in 1873. The slope down from his home at THE LODGE, Lancaster Road, to the foot of Hewthwaite Terrace, became known as FIDDLER'S HILL.

AROUND TOWN

1. Roland Sharp of Market Street was agent for "The CARNFORTH WEEKLY NEWS", which was issued on Saturdays and cost ONE PENNY (240d = £1).

2. J W SMITH, 23 Market Street was advertised as newsagent, stationer, printer, and bill-poster. Large placards pasted to the gable-ends of houses, and onto wooden hoardings around the town, were the chief way for large companies to advertise their products.

3. When people needed wreaths for funerals or wedding bouquets, they went to Cragbank Nurseries run by Mr Len Wrightson. He also specialised in bedding plants, fruit trees etc.

[This early Garden Centre is now a private residence, 182 Lancaster Road.]

4. Doctor E Jackson, whose surgery was at ROBIN HILL in Market Street, was the local surgeon, medical officer and public vaccinator.

5. The firm of HARTLEY'S was prospering at its two local shops. One was in Millhead, and the other at Carnforth's busy crossroads near the Carnforth Inn. They were advertised as FAMILY GROCERS, TEA & COFFEE DEALERS. BISCUIT BAKERS, CONFECTIONERS, CATERERS & FEEDING-STUFF MERCHANTS.

CHURCH EXTENSION

Extensive work was done on CHRIST CHURCH to increase the seating capacity from 328 to 550. The alterations were vitally necessary because of the over-crowding at some services.

It was reported that after Evensong on particular Sundays, some people had become ill and fainted, because of the crush when leaving church. Both front entrances had had to be used.

Our townspeople were strong in their religious faith and the church of each denomination was very well supported.

A large crowd of Primitive Methodists shows how Carnforth was full of religious fervour in the late 19th century.

A MODERN INVENTION

There was great excitement among the children in the playgrounds of the NATIONAL SCHOOL when they heard the approach of a very loud, rattling noise.

Annie Barnham waved and cheered with the other scholars when a strange, horseless carriage called a MOTOR CAR went clattering by on Lancaster Road.

The driver wore a long, cotton coat, a peaked hat secured under his chin and goggles to protect him from the clouds of dust which was disturbed on some roads.

The sort of horseless carriage called a Motor Car *which the children ran out of the playground to see.*

THE CARNFORTH CYCLE CO.

This firm had been established in 1896 at a white-washed building adjoining the CARNFORTH INN. It had been turning out over 100 new cycles per annum, but THE WHEELS OF TIME were turning! The company built the first MOTORCYCLE to be owned in Carnforth in this year 1901, and had started to do MOTOR REPAIRS.

Manager: C Dean.

SCHOOL EXAMS

Samples of my mother's (Annie Barnham) examination papers, done in 1900 and 1901, show extremely neat work. The handwriting in her COPY BOOK is beautiful and her composition on "THRIFT" shows that she was a member of a careful family. Part of her essay reads, "A thrifty person is one who tries to get on and is not lazy ... pays ready money and so gets discount, and saves money so he/she can buy tools if an apprenticeship is to be served ... is sensible and joins clubs and societies so money will come in, even during illness. Some people are poor because they waste things and spend money on useless articles." *[What words of wisdom to pass on to one's descendants!]*

Done in neat figuring, her ARITHMETIC shows quite complicated work with fractions and decimals, and the necessity of a good knowledge of TABLES, including perches, furlongs, poles, etc.

The eldest girls in many large families only received four-fifths of their education at the National School, because every Monday they were kept at home to mind the babies and toddlers whilst their mothers were coping with the heavy weekly wash. As the eldest of six, my mother was amongst the girls who missed out educationally. She said that she would have loved to stay on after reaching the leaving age of 13 and to have become a PUPIL TEACHER.

CARNFORTH DIGNITARIES

The following people were mentioned in a 1901 directory of the district:

WILLIAM PERFECT	Tailor, Bank Buildings
JOHN HIMSWORTH	Grocer, New Street
CHRIS McDONALD	Jeweller, 25 Market Street
ROBERT CARR	Grocer & Beer Retailer, Lancaster Road
ALFRED HOYLE	Station Hotel
MR SLINGER	Farmer, Hodgson's Croft Farm
WILLIAM IRELAND	Farmer, Thwaite Farm
GEORGE RATHBONE	Teacher of Music & Music Dealer, Market Street

BARROW SHIPYARDS

Some Carnforth lads, who belonged to over-large families, had considered joining the Royal Navy to escape from cramped conditions at home. In

October they heard some news which made them have second thoughts The Navy might expect them to sail UNDER the waves instead of on top! Those big cranes at Barrow, which could be clearly seen across the Bay, had been very busy again. Vickers had launched the world's fastest cruiser and the Royal Navy's first SUBMARINE.

The Market Street Music Shop of George Rathbone (Senior). His son, George (brother of Tom), was a gifted musician, whose many works were published by the Ivor Novello Music Corporation.

THE BOER WAR

No sooner had the sad soldier's song, "Good-bye Dolly Grey", become familiar in Carnforth than news arrived of the first British troops returning in triumph from the war on Oct 29th and meeting up with their Dollies again. *[Sadly a second phase of this war broke out eventually.]*

WOMEN SURGEONS?

When it was heard in November that male colleagues had refused to work with a WOMAN house-surgeon in Macclesfield, Dr Jackson's patients declared, "Quite right too! We certainly wouldn't have a woman poking about in our 'innards'!"

SENDING MESSAGES

A young shunter in the L.N.W R. marshalling yards could not shout loud enough to communicate with his friend, digging in his allotment in front of Grosvenor Place. He just couldn't believe that an Italian chap called Marconi had sent a message over 350 miles ... without wires. Incredible! Tell that to a dead donkey!

CANALS

Children liked to stand near the Bank Ranger's Cottage by the CANAL BASIN and watch coal barges from the south being unloaded. Men shovelled the coal into wheelbarrows, which they trundled off into the nearby coal-yard, where it was weighed and put into sacks. Some barrowloads were emptied directly onto high-sided carts, which had been backed into the open square, built into the high wall which separates the canal banks from Lancaster Road. Carnforth coal-merchants then gee-upped their horses and drove off to do their local deliveries.

Whilst all this was going on, the tired barge-horses were unharnessed and led into stables adjoining the cottage, to be fed and rested in readiness for the return journey to Preston, with a load of stones and sand from the gravel-hole at the other side of the canal.

It was back in 1792 that Pinkerton and Murray, the canal construction firm, had started at Tewitfield (Carnforth) to dig the 17 mile stretch to Ellel, which was the first length of the proposed Preston to Kendal canal. The whole 57 miles had not been completed until 1815 because of various engineering problems, such as the building of 8 locks at Tewitfield, the aqueduct over the Lune at Lancaster and the 382 yards long tunnel through a hill near Hincaster.

Kellet Road Canal Bridge (Northern side), Canal Terrace at top right. The Brass Band had a hut alongside the lane of the left which leads to Canal Cottages.

When Carnforthians learnt that Britain and America had just agreed terms for the building of an important shipping canal, they wondered how long that great task would take, bearing in mind the 23 years it had taken to build our Kendal to Preston canal. It was proposed that a waterway should be cut through the narrow neck of land connecting North and South America and thus allow ships to sail directly from the Atlantic to the Pacific Ocean along the Panama Canal. That indeed would be some canal!

[The Bank Ranger's Cottage, the adjoining stables and the loading-bay in the wall facing Hewthwaite Terrace can still be seen near the canal basin.]

Approaching the Canal Basin. Bank Ranger's Cottage on the left. Note the Gas Works in the centre and the 220ft tall Iron Works chimney in the distance.

1902

The most important event in this year was the coronation of the late Queen Victoria's eldest son as King Edward VII and his consort as Queen Alexandra. She was a Danish princess.

Smith's the Newsagents printed leaflets giving details of the events planned for the celebrations. These were to be issued free on the great day, July 26th, but additional copies would cost 1d.

Church service leaflet - Edwards VII's Coronation, 1902.

Grand CORONATION SPORTS were to be held and, to prevent athletic people from other towns and villages coming here and winning all our valuable prizes, the contests were for Carnforth residents only. 1st prizes 3s 0d (15p), 2nd 2s 0d (10p) and 3rd 1s 0d (5p).

Events did not occur as arranged however. On June 24th, just 2 days before the carefully planned celebrations, King Edward was taken desperately ill. He was given an emergency operation for appendicitis in a specially prepared room at Buckingham Palace, and the coronation was postponed indefinitely.

[My mother saved her leaflet about Carnforth's Coronation Day plans and, as far as I know, events here had to go ahead as arranged. HARTLEY'S, our famous local caterers, and other firms too would already have had a lot of food prepared and it would have been unthinkable to waste it.]

Our celebrations were on such a large scale that 4 separate committees had been necessary to complete all the arrangements for:

1. AN OLD FOLK'S DINNER

2. A CHILDREN'S TEA

3. THE PARADE

4. A BONFIRE & FIREWORKS

A full day's programme was planned and proceedings started at 10am with a huge assembly on the MARKET GROUND. Led by the BRASS BAND, the FIRE BRIGADE and our COUNCILLORS, a large Church Parade set off up MARKET STREET and each denomination, headed by its own minister, made its way to its CHURCH.

Services were held at 10.30 and afterwards the Brass Band met the Wesleyans, proceeded along Lancaster Rood, where the Church of England worshippers fell in, and then moved on to the crossroads and collected the people from the Congregational Church. The large crowd then halted at the MARKET GROUND and sang the National Anthem with patriotic fervour, led by Councillor Rigg.

At noon, 'THE OLD FOLK' sat down to an excellent dinner in the STATION HOTEL'S VICTORIA HALL.

An enormous crowd of adults and children assembled on the MARKET GROUND at 1.30pm ready for a GRAND PROCESSION to set off around Carnforth at 2pm.

Children were marshalled according to ages and each carried a small Union Jack, as requested. The National Anthem was sung and then the Brass Band led the parade, followed by:

1. Girls

2. THE SALVATION ARMY BAND

3. Boys

4. THE FIRE BRIGADE

5. The Boys' Brigade with its band

6. All Carnforth's Friendly Societies

7. A turn-out of Tradesmen's Vehicles.

After the tour of our main streets, the parade headed up North Road to the Sports Field.

From 3 - 3.45, the Brass Band played a programme of patriotic melodies whilst judging took place of the Tradesmen's vehicles, and sports for boys and girls were held.

At 3.45 there was BUGLE CALL for the Children's Teas and presentation of CORONATION MUGS. To prevent a host of fussy mothers interfering the serving of teas ("My Little Willie only likes cakes with PINK icing on them" etc. etc.) no one was allowed inside the enclosure except the members of the TEA COMMITTEE and their assistants. (How wise!)

To give the Brass Band musicians time to have a rest and "wet their whistles", the SALVATION ARMY BAND kept the music going until the sports were resumed. The Brass Band then carried on with oom-pa-pas until 6pm.

The evening's jollifications started off at 7.30 in the playground of the National School, with competitions for comic costumes in the CYCLE PARADE. The prizes for the best decorated machines make interesting reading:

GENTS PRIZES

1st: Pair of pictures (value 10s 6d (52.5p)

2nd: Pair of cricket pants (value 7s 6d (37.5p)

3rd: A fishing rod (value 5 6d (27.5p)

LADIES PRIZES

1st: Umbrella (10s 6d)

2nd: Groceries (7s 6d)

3rd: Camera (5s 6d)

There were classes for children too.

At 8pm there was a GRAND CYCYLE PARADE around the town:

1. The Band

2. LADY CYCLISTS

3. FIRE BRIGADE

4. GENTLEMAN CYCLISTS

They went down NEW STREET, up MARKET STREET, along LANCASTER ROAD to the top of HEWTHWAITE TERRACE, then turned back and went up NORTH ROAD to ALMA TERRACE, down to BANK CORNER and up LANCASTER ROAD, back to the NATIONAL SCHOOL.

At 9.55pm A SIGNAL ROCKET whooshed up into the sky and at 10pm THE NATIONAL ANTHEM was sung (AGAIN!), the huge BONFIRE was lit and there was a beautiful display of FIREWORKS.

This special day of celebrations was concluded with a WONDERFUL WATER CARNIVAL on the canal.

What a memorable day of interesting and enjoyable events in which ALL Carnforth's inhabitants could take part. Not even the HORSES were forgotten! Be they 'HEAVY' or 'LIGHT', our ever-useful animals could join in. They were on parade around the STATION HOTEL at 1.30pm, competing for prizes as "THE BEST DRESSED HORSE" or PAIR (in top-hat, white tie and tails??)

Prizes, as in all the day's events, were willingly donated by our local personalities, who were proud to be good Carnforthians. Our town was a colourful red-white-and-blue picture, with flags and bunting in all our streets. Prizes had been awarded to the best decorated premises, according to their rateable value: £7, £10, £13, or £13+ per annum.

[This memorable and joyous occasion has been recorded in some detail to show how efficient and self-sufficient Carnforth was in providing pleasure for ALL its inhabitants without the aid of famous people from other places, and with NO canned entertainment of any sort.

Nowadays, almost 100 years later, would Carnforthians be willing and able to celebrate some great event in such a united, patriotic and happy way? At the time of writing, THE MILLENNIUM is not far from distant!]

THE CORONATION . . . Eventually

On August 9th EDWARD VII was crowned king in Westminster Abbey in his 60th year. The ceremony had to take a shortened form because HIS HIGHNESS was still not fully restored to health.

LAW BREAKING

In spite of the cold dark weather, lots of giggles were heard on Jan 9th when the young people of Carnforth read in the newspapers that the city of New York had introduced a bill to stop public flirting.

"Our English law-makers had better not try to stop us from winking at the handsome young men serving behind the counters in the Co-op grocers!" said some bold lasses, out shopping down New Street.

QUARRYING

Many roads and railways were being built throughout Britain, and this led to a big demand for sand, gravel and stones, which our Carnforth area had in abundance due to glacial movements during the Ice Age.

After the Industrial Revolution, the many quarries dug here and there scarred the beauty of our countryside, but gave employment for quite a number of men in the locality. Canal barges bringing coal northward carried loads of sand and gravel on the return journeys to the southern end of our canal.

People were reminded of the dangers of quarry work when they heard in the spring that a worker had been crushed to death in the gravel-hole near Carnforth railway station. Over the years, bones, skulls and whole skeletons had been dug up there, sometimes only a couple of feet below the surface.

THE END OF THE BOER WAR

After 2 years and 7 months, the war in South Africa finally end on May 3rd. It had been the first time that photographers, film cameramen and war correspondents had gone into battle with the troops, and what they saw came as a shock. Carnforth people did not see them because our town did not have a cinema, but pictures and accounts in newspapers told of bungled battles and deadly outbreaks of dysentery.

The Government took no care of maimed and wounded troops, and there was great poverty and suffering among families who had lost their bread-winner. Various charities and well-known personalities did their best to help. Dedicated to those in distress, Rudyard Kipling wrote a poem entitled "THE ABSENT-MINDED BEGGAR", which was featured on various forms of memorabilia and some of them were on sale at McDONALD'S SHOP in Market Street.

[My mother bought a cup and saucer which she treasured all her life.]

CRICKET

Cricket enthusiasts among the people on their way to the Post Office in Station Buildings were interested in a large poster which had been pasted on the wooden hoardings at the bottom of Market Street. It was a COLEMAN'S MUSTARD advertisement featuring that famous cricketer Dr W G Grace.

Of course he was an excellent player, but our First Eleven who played on the cricket field behind Hewthwaite Terrace would have given him a run for his money. Among our team were those popular tradesmen HARRY GILL, Mr RIGG, Mr COLLINGE & Mr HIMSWORTH.

PARCEL SERVICE

William Barnham, 39 HIGHFIELD TERRACE, liked the idea of being a pioneer in some sphere or other. When he read in the Daily Mail on Aug 10th that the London Post Office had sent its first parcel mail to the USA on the White Star Liner *Teutonic*, he'd felt he'd missed a good opportunity by not getting off a package to his sister Ada, who had emigrated and was living in Duluth.

POLITICS

Carnforth Conservatives had an excellent club which had been opened in 1887 in Station Buildings. It had a well-equipped billiards and reading room. Britain had a Conservative Government and Arthur Balfour had recently taken over as Prime Minister from his uncle Lord Salisbury.

The Liberals had a strong following here so, not to be outdone, they too had opened a club in 1887. It was in a building at the top right-hand side of Stanley Street (now a laundrette).

There was no Labour Party, but Carnforth men with leanings towards Socialism were interested in reports of a speech given in London by a Scotsman named Keir Hardie. A month later they learnt that the Trades Union Congress had voted to form a central organisation to get Labour candidates into Parliament and to advise them after winning seats. Perhaps Carnforth would have a Labour Club some time in the future.

THE BAND OF HOPE

Meetings of Carnforth's BAND OF HOPE were held in the school room under the Wesleyan Chapel on Lancaster Road.

The movement strove to keep young people from succumbing to the temptation of STRONG DRINK.

Annie Barnham, age 14, of Highfield Terrace won a

beautiful CERTIFICATE OF MERIT presented by the Lancashire and Cheshire Band of Hope and Temperance for the excellence of her written report of a lecture on "ALCOHOL AND THE HUMAN BODY" *[an enthralling topic!]*

GETTING SHAVED

Beards were going out of fashion and shaving became a daily chore for most men. It was a difficult and dangerous task performed by candle-light in front of a tiny mirror hanging over the back kitchen slopstone. A shaving brush was dipped into an enamel mug full of hot water, vigorously rubbed on a stick of shaving-soap and then lathered onto the face. A lethal cut-throat razor was then carefully guided to remove the foam and the whiskers, whilst leaving the nose in its correct position. A blunt razor meant a painful shave so it had to be kept sharp on a leather 'strop' hooked on to the back door.

It was good news when newspapers reported that a man called Gillette was marketing a replaceable razor which was designed to be used just once, or until blunt. It was hoped that it wouldn't be long before that invention reached Carnforth.

FASHIONS FOR FEMALES

Victorian fashions were changing. Bustles and tightly-laced corsets were being discarded and hemlines were slowly creeping above the ankle. Styles which allowed for more freedom at work and at play were welcomed, but none of Carnforth's lady cyclists were bold enough to venture forth on the streets wearing those daring knickerbockers favoured by a female named BLOOMER.

1903

A FURNESS RAILWAY DISASTER

During the stormy night of Feb 27th, TOM SHAW of HILL STREET was driving the 5.25am train from Cark when disaster struck on LEVEL VIADUCT. The gale blew the carriages on to their sides but the engine remained upright. About 50 terrified passengers struggled free and, clinging to the metal, they crawled to safety through the darkness and the 100mph winds.

Thomas Shaw of Hill Street, Carnforth was the driver of the ill-fated train.

OVER-CROWDING

Accommodation was very cramped for large families of 10, 11, 12 and even 17 who lived in two-up-two-down houses such as those in HILL STREET, RAMSDEN STREET, POND STREET, RUSSELL ROAD, lower HIGHFIELD TERRACE etc. As new babies continued to arrive, it was essential for the oldest children to move out. Boys who did not want to become farm-workers joined the Army or Navy.

Bright girls could stay on at the National School or the British School and train as PUPIL TEACHERS. The alternative for those not so academically gifted was to go into SERVICE at a local farm or be a live-in servant for one of Carnforth's better-off families.

NEW JOBS

There was wonderful news for the young ladies of Carnforth when a poster appeared in the window of a newsagent's shop in Market Street. It invited females to apply for jobs as machinists at a mill which J. D. RAMSAY & CO. LTD, clothes manufacturers of Kendal, had built in the yard of RIGGS THE CONTRACTORS at the bottom of OXFORD STREET. One side of the new building ran across the back streets of Oxford Street and Stanley Street.

The type of garment made at Morphy's Mill. The girls were paid a few shillings for sewing a dozen garments.

My mother Annie, aged 15, was nearly the first of the young ladies, who eagerly applied for the 35 – 40 positions available because they considered the work would be much better than going "into service".

A present-day photograph of the side wall of Morphy's Mill, which runs along the bottom of Stanley Street and Oxford Street backs.

ENTERTAINMENT

The only picture-shows to be seen in Carnforth were those to be enjoyed at BAND OF HOPE meetings. A "MAGIC LANTERN" shone slides onto a screen and some adult with abstemious habits gave a commentary. The stories were always a warning against ALCOHOL, and told of drunken fathers battering their families and causing poverty and suffering.

People were intrigued when they read in their newspapers that a MOVING FILM had been made. It was called "THE GREAT TRAIN ROBBERY", and lasted for 8 minutes. In it the bandit chief fired a pistol at point-blank range toward the terrified audience causing panic.

Carnforth could do without entertainment like that! (Nurses had to be in attendance at some of those early 'movies'.)

THE READING ROOM

The Co-operative Wholesale Society had a READING ROOM at the top of their premises in New Street. It was reached by a doorway in JOHN STREET, which opened onto a steep spiral staircase. The ante-room of the large Co-op Hall was on the first floor, and the READING ROOM was up on the second floor.

Various newspapers and magazines were displayed on a large table around which were chairs with wooden arms, and the room was heated by an open coal fire.

Only MEN used the room and they were indignant when they read that a female named Emmeline Pankhurst had formed a militant movement to gain votes for WOMEN. The very idea! What could women possibly know about politics?

More surprising knowledge was learnt in that reading room. Someone called Madame Curie had become the first woman to win THE NOBEL PRIZE IN PHYSICS. Her studies concerned the mystery of radioactivity.

The fact that the 'NATIONAL SOCIETY FOR THE PREVENTION OF CRUELTY TO CHILDREN' had opened in headquarters in London was the subject for many discussions. Carnforth needed no Cruelty Inspectors! Parents loved their children even though they walloped them when necessary. Policemen, teachers and even neighbours sometimes disciplined them but, at the same time, kept an affectionate, protective eye on them.

FLYING MACHINES

In December Mr Dan Miller, the Headmaster, told his pupils that, at Kitty Hawk in America, the WRIGHT BROTHERS, Wilbur and Orville, had recently flown a heavier-than-air machine. They had made 4 flights and the longest had lasted for almost one minute and covered 850ft! The only things that the children had seen flying in the air over Carnforth were butterflies, birds and winged insects of many varieties.

AN ATLANTIC CROSSING

The Cunard Liner, LUSITANIA, sailed across the Atlantic Ocean in five and a half days, and was the first liner to communicate from mid-Atlantic with wireless stations on both sides of the ocean.

Perhaps there was a couple of young Carnforth

men aboard, fleeing to a new life overseas because they had got girls INTO TROUBLE.

Mr Smith, the newsagent in Market Street, was our town's EMIGRATION OFFICER and he could have arranged matters for them. A London Transatlantic liner ticket cost £6 for 3rd class travel.

INTERNAL COMBUSTION ENGINES

No one owned a car in Carnforth and few were to be seen on our main road, but it was reported in newspapers that motor traffic was increasing in cities. Parliament was considering a new law to have vehicles registered and numbered. County Councils would fix speed limits, but it was decided drivers need not past tests and there would be no penalties for drunken drivers.

1903 Standard
Downhill, and with a following wind
it topped 25 M.P.H.

CARNFORTH URBAN DISTRICT COUNCIL

Statement of Accounts for year ended March 1903.

Money had to be spent on the upkeep of our roads because of the number of cars travelling through the town. Maintenance of the Highway cost the huge sum of £88 12s 0d. Another £28 12s 0d was spent on secondary roads, and street improvements cost £7 16s 3d.

Other interesting expenses were as follows:

a. SEWERAGE - £16 7s 6d

b. SCAVENGING & WATERING STREETS - £82 19s 11d *(Streets needed washing down because tradesmen were no successful in toilet-training their horses)*

c. PUBLIC LIGHTING - £140 2s 10d *(The electricity bill for ONE family would cost more today)*

d. MARKET GROUND - £4 4s 6d

e. HOSPITAL (at Cragbank) - £332 18s 0d

f. FIRE BRIGADE - £27 4s 6d

g. PUBLIC OFFICES - £36 11s 3d

h. ELECTION EXPENSES - £17 6s 5d

i. SALARIES OF OFFICERS - £132 19s 8d *(It is wondered how many officers shared out the £2 11s 0d weekly amount?)*

j. REMOVAL OF ASHES - £90 0s 0d *(It seems that for emptying smelly EARTH CLOSETS, 2 men and a horse shared around £1 14s between them each week!)*

k. CORONATION EXPENSES - £94 15s 6d

THE GENERAL DISTRICT RATE brought in £1282 19s 5d to meet the expenses and the balance in the treasurer's hands at the end of the year was £279 19s 5d.

[Two householders may now pay more rates than all of Carnforth in 1903]

1904

CHRIST CHURCH

The death of the church's second vicar, the Rev Edwards Scott (appointed in 1877) caused sadness in the parish.

He was succeeded by the Rev Clive Muir.

THE CARNFORTH INN

Described as an 'ancient hostelry' in an old directory, this building had been erected in 1620.

This year it had alterations and extensions, and from being a rectangular inn facing Lancaster Road, it became L-shaped and formed the corner with Market Street. The addition of a roofed veranda gave the frontage a smart appearance.

OUR BRASS BAND

Carnforth was proud of the band, which played a melodious part in all our town's special events.

The bandsmen welcomed new uniforms: peaked hats, single-breasted suits with smart shoulder-and-cuff trimmings, and broad white bands worn diagonally across the chest.

TOBACCO TAX

Next door to the Post Office in Station Buildings was the shop of Ben Adamson, Hairdresser and

High Class Tobacconist.

He was an umbrella and walking-stick specialist and his shop had hair-cutting, shaving and shampooing rooms.

He had a lot of grumbling, disgruntled customers in April, because Austen Chamberlain's first budget had announced that a 3d per lb duty was to be put on tobacco. Carnforth's many pipe smokers were enraged and the president of the Tobacco Retailers declared that the last 6 years had been enough to drive Britain's tax-hit tobacconists into a lunatic asylum. Poor Ben Adamson!

MODERN INVENTIONS

1. In February, the great opera star, CARUSO, had his voice recorded, and thanks to his phonograph, future generations would be able to enjoy his singing. The news fell on deaf ears in Carnforth as no one had a phonograph.

2. The news that Charles Rolls and Henry Royce had merged their companies to produce wonderful Rolls Royce cars also left our inhabitants quite unimpressed. No railwayman or worker at the Iron-works owned a car ... or would ever be likely to have one!

3. In March there was consternation among the young engine-cleaners busily at work in the 'Wessie' sheds (L.N.W.R.), when they heard that a main line train had run from Liverpool to

Southport, not powered by steam, but by that mysterious invention, ELECTRICITY.

4. Some of our scientifically-minded young men, who had been experimenting with unreliable crystal-and-cats'-whisker combinations, were very interested to learn of the invention of a new valve which looked rather like an electric light bulb and would make the operation of wireless-receivers much less frustrating.

5. Less puzzling for the mind was the news that Manchester City had beaten Bolton Wanderers 1-0 in the F.A. Cup match at Crystal Palace. Cheers!

AN ACCIDENT AT THE MILL

On August 16th James Ramsey & Co, clothing manufacturers, were charged in court for allowing the driving-shaft of machinery at their premises in Rigg's Yard to go unguarded. They were fined £1.

My mother Annie Barnham, a machinist aged 16, had left her seat to pick up some scraps of material from the floor near the shaft. As was the fashion for all young unmarried ladies, her long hair was tied back with a bow of ribbon. As she bent down it swung into the machinery and half of it was painfully riven from her scalp.

The report of the case, which appeared in the Lancaster Guardian, stated that young Annie had been reprimanded for leaving her seat on a Tuesday. SATURDAY was tidying-up day!

[90 years later I came across an article in 'BELLA' magazine about an almost identical accident. This time the young lady was awarded £1000 damages and her employers were fined £1000 plus a further £1000 for costs. She was given months off work to recover. Her workmates clapped and cheered when she resumed her job. TIMES HAD CHANGED! Trade Unions had come into being.

My mother often told me about her terrible ordeal; she was 'head-sore' for the rest of her life. How she must have suffered, not only physically but also emotionally, in those days when a woman's hair was regarded as her CROWNING GLORY.]

POSTCARDS

Along with the rest of Britain, Carnforthians acquired a craze for COLLECTING POSTCARDS. It had become fashionable to send postcards when on holiday. Postage was ½d, so 480 could be posted for £1.

Carnforth was a centre for holiday-makers who loved the beauty of the countryside, so the cards posted here were mostly pictures of our local beauty spots. People on seaside holidays at places like Morecambe and Blackpool enjoyed sending very saucy cards to their friends.

The message on cards often started off with the words, "ONE MORE FOR YOUR COLLECTION". Some people just kept their cards in albums, but others, with more original ideas, glued them to tall screens and then applied a coat of varnish over them. (Screens were useful draught-excluders in homes which only had a fire in one room). Some artistic folk used their card collections to decorate big brown earthen-ware pipes, as used underground in water and sewage works. The finished pipes looked very attractive when stood upright and used as stands for umbrellas and walking-sticks - both necessary for well-turned out ladies and gentleman.

A fanciful image of **Carnforth-by-the-sea!**

Annie Barnham treasured all the postcards sent to her by her sweetheart, Tom Wilkinson, during their long courtship. Many of them, bearing views of railway stations - CREWE, CARLISLE, STAFFORD, ST. HELENS etc. - were written to cancel one of their appointments when he had unexpectedly had to 'book-off on a double trip' in the course of his duties as a fireman on the footplate of a L.N.W.R. locomotive.

[Birthday & Christmas cards of the time were very collectable. Made of celluloid, some were embossed with prettily coloured hearts, flowers & leaves. Tom, my father, was no Romeo with a pen! In his well-formed handwriting he stated with no display of passion: TO ANNIE FROM TOM.

Postcards had originated in Austria in 1869 as plain pieces of card with a pre-printed stamp.

When pictorial cards had been introduced in 1894, one side was reserved for the address, with the picture on the reverse.

The use of cards rocketed, and the years from then until the start of World War I became known as THE GOLDEN AGE OF POSTCARDS.]

MOTOR CARS

Between the manager and his workmen at Carnforth's Motor Company, there was speculation about RELIABLE, light cars which would sell for a huge sum of money, between £150 – £200.

There were reports that the machines were a big improvement on the HORSE, and faster in cities. Drivers of the motors would no longer need to be mechanics, because of the simple design and construction of the vehicles. The hazards of breakdowns would be cut. How exciting it would be if some rich person in our locality decided to own one!

1905

After the construction of Carnforth's main buildings and streets in the 1880s and 1890s there was little growth, and gaps between houses in some areas were not filled in - along Lancaster and Scotland Roads, Preston and Hawk Streets, for instance.

The house adjoining the CHURCH ROOM in Preston Street was occupied by the caretaker. The space between that house and the one at the top was never filled in, although alternate stones had been left projecting at the front side of each in anticipation of further building.

The Iron Works viewed from the hillside above Scotland Rd.

When the IRON WORKS had been working at top capacity, it had been thought that Carnforth might grow rapidly to the size of Barrow. Now, that seemed highly unlikely.

DALE GROVE'S two houses had been built in 1901. Numbers 1 & 2 MORNINGSIDE were built at the top of Hewthwaite Terrace in 1905, and KING STREET and ALEXANDRA ROAD were named in honour of the new king and queen.

Crewdson's Fish and Chipped Potatoe Saloon*, top left house in Hunter Street.*

The following streets, terraces and roads now formed the nucleus of our town:

The Row, The Drive, Cragbank Lane, Hope Terrance, Travellers' Rest, Dale Grove, The Nurseries, Hall Street, Hewthwaite Terrace, Fern Bank, Alexandra Road, King Street, Stanley Street, Hill Street, Lancaster Road, Lower North Road, Canal Bridge Houses, Kellet Road, Annas Bank,

Highfield Terrace, Russell Road, Alma Terrace, Market Street, Scotland Road, New Street, Preston Street, Edward Street, Haws Hill, Booth Street, Grosvenor Place, Hunter Street, Ramsden Street, Pond Street, Pond Terrace, Station Buildings, Midland Terrace, Kerr Villas and Shore Lane.

THE SALVATION ARMY

Back in 1886, a group of Carnforth people had been fired with enthusiasm when they heard the teaching of the Salvation Army Movement, under its General, William Booth. They had wanted to join 'GOD's ARMY' in its battle against THE DEMON DRINK, which was causing poverty, cruelty and crime throughout the land. A corps was founded and services were held in a room above a stable on spare land behind Hunter St.

Horses belonging to Dockray's, the Corn and Seed merchants (lower Preston Street), were kept in the lower part of the building.

The number of Salvation Army 'soldiers' in Carnforth grew rapidly and it was necessary to have larger quarters. These were built in Preston Street, partly of corrugated iron with a good brick frontage. Soon the corps had an excellent marching band, which helped to spread the Salvation Army message all round town.

1904 had proved to be a great year for the Movement. The first meeting of the International S.A. Congress had been held, and William Booth, the General, had completed a Crusading Trip from Land's End to Aberdeen.

In 1905, the distinguished-looking leader, with a long white beard, started off again, this time on a 2000 mile motor-crusade. He left Dover on his 10 week mission to spark a countrywide flame of religious fervour.

At the crossroads here, a huge crowd assembled to see and hear him when his remarkable white car stopped outside the CARNFORTH INN *[which we can rest assured he did NOT enter to partake of liquid refreshment].*

Among the tightly-packed crowd of people, ALL wearing hats, were our local Salvationists, proudly holding their banners aloft.

LEISURE TIME

After a 12-hour day of hard work at the Iron Works, in a quarry or on the railway, our workmen liked to escape from a house full of boisterous children on dark evenings. Off they would go to join their friends at their LOCAL: THE CARNFORTH INN, THE QUEEN'S HOTEL, THE SHOVEL INN, THE CROSS KEYS or THE TRAVELLERS' REST.

(The latter two were classed as BEER HOUSES and did not originally have licences to sell wines and spirits, which were not workmen's tipples anyway). Those men going to the select STATION HOTEL were served only at the SAW DUST END.

[Drunkenness which caused poverty was a problem of the times.]

Ladies did NOT go to 'pubs' - that would have been shameful!

Elegant ladies outside the old Carnforth Inn near the bank-corner crossroads.

Mothers with young families were tied to the home, but those with older children who were able to mind their young siblings, could occasionally have a night out, of a genteel nature.

'SEWING Bs' became popular with the ladies of the various churches. Clever needle-work produced items for BAZAARS and SALES-OF-WORK, and the jolly chit-chat enjoyed by the ladies was extremely therapeutic - NO malicious gossip was allowed of course!

The Parish Church group arrived at the Vicarage, wearing an eye-catching array of very large flower-bedecked hats, smart 'boaters' or feather and lace-trimmed black bonnets. Veils and hat-pins were in vogue and helped to keep unruly head-gear anchored firmly to the head.

MEDICATION

ASPIRINS for the relief of pain were on sale for the first time in English cities. Some doctors were concerned that the tablets could cause stomach trouble, sweating and sickness. A hospital professor decided that they would be useful in countering headaches due to anxiety and over-work.

Stocks would arrive, eventually, at No. 30 Market Street, the chemist's shop owned by J P Porteus, because he advertised "PATENT MEDICINES and PURE DRUGS" (Pure?). Until then people would have to continue with the old Carnforth remedy - a piece of old sheeting soaked in an enamel basin containing vinegar and water and then applied to the forehead of the patient, whilst he/she lay in a recumbent posture in a bedroom darkened by pulling down the green blind, which was essential for night-workmen.

CANAL DANGERS

Children were warned to behave sensibly on the canal banks, especially when walking under bridges. There was an extremely dangerous spot which must be avoided and that was the place on the basin where a large underground pipe carried water from the canal to the railway yards. There, water towers were kept topped-up for filling the boilers of locomotive engines.

A FALLACY

Government figures showed an increase in RURAL LUNACY owing to the tedium of country life.

[Carnforth tedious? NEVER! There was always lots going on.]

Trippers enjoying the sea breeze.

SEASIDE OUTINGS

Holiday excursions by train to seaside places became very popular, and Carnforth station was a busy place. Passengers travelling on the Furness or Midland Line need not use the station's main entrance. Nearly opposite to the Post Office at the end of Station Buildings was a metal turn-stile, which gave access to a flight of stone steps leading down to the forecourt of the station's entrance on Warton Road. Special trains were put on to carry the holiday crowds.

How Carnforth ladies looked when paddling in the sea on an outing to Blackpool.

At seaside holiday resorts, bathing machines could be hired. They were towed into the sea by horses as the occupants changed into bathing costumes with sleeves and long legs, which kept most of their bodies discreetly concealed. Day-trippers from Carnforth to Morecambe, Southport or Blackpool could not afford such luxury. They were quite content to paddle their feet in the sea, having firstly pinned-up their long skirts, taking great care not to show too much leg.

BALLOONS

Carnforth children loved gaily-coloured balloons, which they bought at INGHAM'S TOY & FANCY GOODS shop in Market Street. They were astounded when they were told that two Frenchman had flown across the English Channel IN A BALLOON and had landed at the Crystal Palace. "However had they managed to do that?" wondered the children.

OUR HOSPITAL

The first child was admitted to the new ISOLATION HOSPITAL at Crag Bank. She was the 6 year-old daughter of Mr and Mrs Howie, who for many years lived with their large family at 14 Hill Street.

The hospital was a building of corrugated iron and stood at the top of a slope alongside SHORE LANE. It had 2 wards in which children suffering from diphtheria or scarlet ever were kept in isolation, away from their brothers and sisters, for 6 weeks ... but sometimes sadly for ever.

MOTOR VEHICLES

The Automobile Association was formed. It helped motorists to avoid wide-spreading speed traps. The legal speed limit was 20mph and police used stopwatches to estimate car speeds. Carnforth 'bobbies' kept on the alert. They were not going to have reckless drivers racing through our town at such a breath-taking speed and endangering the lives of the inhabitants.

London had its first motorised ambulance service for traffic-accident victims. Our ambulance travelled at a more leisurely pace, pulled by Dockray's horses. John Dockray, Corn and Flour Merchant and Hay and Straw Dealer, sold all kinds of foods for horses, cattle, poultry and dogs. The warehouse was at the corner of Haws Hill and Lower Preston Street. Carts were backed between the wide doors and a rope pulley was used to lift and lower sacks to the second and third floors.

THRIFT

The Board of Education called for the encouragement of great THRIFT among children. Headmaster, Dan Miller, had been teaching the benefits of the economy for several years *[re. my mother's essay on Thrift]* so the Government was behind the times as far as Carnforth was concerned.

Opposite the Wesleyan Chapel, at the junction of Lancaster Road with New Street, THOMPSON'S had a shop and offices, which were the headquarters for an extensive Pawn-broking business with shops in numerous towns. The well-known sign of the "Three Golden Balls" did not hang over the Carnforth shop - the inhabitants did not pawn their possessions. The saying, "Money is made round to go round", was disputed here. The local version was, "Money is made flat, to stack".

Looking down New Street from Lancaster Road. Co-op premises on the right, Iron Works chimney in the distance. Thompson's Brokery business once on the left.

SONGS AND NAMES

The song hits of the year were:

"HOW'D YOU LIKE TO SPOON WITH ME?" and "WAIT TILL THE SUN SHINES, NELLIE!"

[Why were people singing to Nellie, whose Christian name was way down at number 23 in the list of the 50 most popular girls' names in the early 1900s?]

The top 12 favourite names for girls were:

Florence, Mary, Alice, Annie, Elsie, Edith, Elizabeth, Doris, Dorothy, Ethel, Gladys, Lillian.

And the boys:

William, John, George, Thomas, Charles, Frederick, Arthur, James, Albert, Ernest, Robert, Henry.

Pleasant rural scene at the top of North Road, formerly the Old Coach Road.

1906

CARNFORTH'S TERRACED HOUSES

The downstairs accommodation in most of the two-bedroomed houses, such as 13 Hill Street, was equally divided between the living room and the kitchen, thus forming two 'TIDY-SIZED' rooms. The front door opened onto a tiny square at the front of the stairs, with the door to the front room at one side (no hall or passage-way). In this living room was a large, iron fire-range with a deep recess at each side. Into one was built a floor-to-ceiling wooden fitment with shelves for crockery and food-stuffs in a cupboard at the top, and three large drawers below.

In the back kitchen was a shallow, brown slopstone with a cold water tap above it, and built into one corner was an iron set-boiler, with a small fire grate below, to heat water in to the 'copper' on WASHING DAYS. There were some open shelves along the walls, and doorways - one leading out into the backyard, and the other to a flight of open, wooden steps descending to a dark cellar. Openings in the grate which covered the coal hole provided the only gleams of light.

For families consisting of boys and girls, sleeping arrangements in just two bedrooms could be difficult. Sometimes a sheet slung over a rope was used as a room divider.

In 3-bedroomed terraced houses (e.g. 39 Highfield

Terrace), it was the downstairs accommodation which caused most inconvenience. They had a passageway downstairs and a landing upstairs. THE PARLOUR with a small tiled fire-place, and the LIVING ROOM with a big iron range, were about the same size. The back-kitchen, however, was very small. Its sink and set-boiler left 'no room to swing a cat', yet places had to be found for a big wringing-machine (the mangle), two wooden dolly-tubs and the 'dolly-legs'.

The parlour (or sitting room) was a waste of good space, because it was only used for family gatherings at Christmas-time and for weddings and funerals. A corpse could lie there peacefully however. Coffins were a problem for 6 or 7 days in two-up-two-down homes with narrow twisting stairs!

Almost all terrace houses were rented. Riggs the Builders and Contractors had built Hill Street, and were the landlords, collecting around half-a-crown weekly (2s 6d - 12½p). Carnforth Co-op bought up a lot of property, and members could pay amounts each week to the Cottage Fund, until the houses were eventually their own. The signs on empty houses said TO LET, not FOR SALE.

To rent to its employees, the Railway Company built terraces of brick (e.g. Grosvenor Place and Midland Terrace) but the rest of Carnforth was mostly built of stone.

Grosvenor Place, built for employees of the LNWR. Each had an allotment. At one time the family in the first house had 17 children.

A POLITICAL EARTHQUAKE

In February our Conservative and Liberal Club-rooms were hives of activity because an election was going on, due to the fact that the Conservative Prime Minister, Arthur Balfour, had lost his Parliamentary seat. Carnforthians probably went to the National School on Lancaster Road to vote.

The Liberals, under Sir Henry Campbell-Bannerman, had a landslide victory:

	Seats Before	**Seat Now**
Liberals	183	399
Conservatives	401	156
(LRC)	2	29

England now had a Liberal Party Government with 3 bright sparks namely Messrs ASQUITH, LLOYD

GEORGE and CHURCHILL (Winston).

There were scenes of rejoicing outside the Liberal Club in Stanley Street, and the people with leanings towards Socialism were heartened when they noted that the Labour Movement was beginning to grow.

MOUNTAINS

The mountains of Cumberland, when viewed across Morecambe Bay, presented Carnforth with scenes of outstanding beauty.

Scafell Pike, Shiddaw, Helvellyn, Great Gable, Coniston Old Man and other hills in the Cumbrian Group were quiet and peaceful and gave England no trouble at all. Not so some dangerous mountains in other countries! In Italy, one named Vesuvius had erupted in April, destroying a village and sending a river of fire towards Naples, where it killed over 100 people. The weight of cinders on roofs caused buildings to collapse.

Later in the month, our King Edward VII visited the scenes of devastation and sympathised with the sad Italians.

Praise be to God we have no volcanoes! Later in the month, we were again reminded of dangers facing foreigners. We enjoyed grumbling about our changeable weather, but EARTHQUAKES we had NOT. Carnforthians were sad to read in their newspapers that a major earthquake had destroyed San Francisco in the USA, killing at least 1000 and causing a fire storm which reduced hundreds of damaged houses to ashes.

THE DANGERS OF PUBLIC HOUSES

In an address to a meeting of Wesleyans, David Lloyd-George stated that, although Britain was the richest country under the sun, it had 10 million workmen living in chronic destitution. It was his opinion that 60% of poverty was caused by DRINKING and GAMBLING. In May, a Government Committee expressed grave concern at what it called THE VAGRANT ARMY of the poor.

Like most places, Carnforth had more PUBS than churches, and unfortunately some men who frequented them squandered what should have been the family house-keeping money, and not only on the DEVIL DRINK. Undercover GAMBLING went on, with bookies' runners surreptitiously collecting betting slips and paying out winnings (less frequently!) There is no wonder that religious people called our pubs DENS OF INIQUITY, and thought lessons should be learnt from the many tramps who trailed along our Highway.

The problems caused by too much alcohol being drunk were nothing like as bad in Carnforth as in big towns and cities, but they worried the organisers of the BAND OF HOPE, who strove to teach young people about the dangers of over-indulgence.

LOCAL TALKING POINTS

1. The Carnforth Cycle Company began to hire out motorcars.

2. A report in the Lancaster Guardian stated that the telephone communication between Carnforth and Morecambe had been opened.

3. Local sportspeople were very interested to learn that the Olympic Games were to be held in Greece after 2000 yrs.

MERRY-GO-ROUNDS

At the County Police Court on July 17th, WILLIAM MURHPY, a Roundabout and Show Proprietor, was charged with causing a nuisance by playing a steam organ on the MARKET GROUND! Most people gave a hearty welcome to travelling fairs, because they brought fun and excitement into Carnforth, but of course there were some long-faced kill-joys around, who considered all forms of enjoyment as sinful.

BUSES?

It was learnt that BUSES were being banned for being too noisy in London. There were 750 rattling around the streets and 400 more were on order, but Carnforth had "none o' them thur 'ere." Trains were cheap and convenient for Hest Bank, Lancaster, Morecambe, Kendal, Silverdale, Grange etc. and people liked to stretch their legs and stride out to nearby villages: Warton, the Kellets etc.

DIETS

Carnforth people enjoyed eating what they liked and what they could afford. Little attention was paid to such things as diets. Living up to the principle of 'WASTE NOT, WANT NOT', it was important that, at meal-times, all plates must be 'cleaned-up'.

The decision about diets among doctors at Guy's Hospital gave people food for thought. It had been known for a century that fresh fruit could prevent scurvy, but recently it had been learnt that a diet of polished rice could lead to beri-beri, curable by eating rice with husks. Fruit and rice husks also contain some still-unidentified material essential for nutrition, for curing scurvy and beri-beri, and possibly for preventing rickets, which was fairly common amongst toddlers in poor families, causing weak bow legs. The doctors concluded that BAD DIETS AS WELL AS GERMS MAY CAUSE SERIOUS DISEASES. That information gave Carnforth minds something to chew over.

VOTES FOR WOMEN

Caring mothers had stocked-up precious ingredients for weeks and weeks, and then tired themselves out making puddings, cakes, mince-pies etc. to put on festive meals for their families at Christmas-time.

When they read in their Daily Mails on Dec 30th that SYLVIA and EMMELINE PANKHURST had refused their Christmas dinners in Holloway Prison, the mothers and FATHERS had little sympathy for those leaders of THE SUFFRAGETTE MOVEMENT who were trying valiantly to get VOTES FOR WOMEN. "It's a pity they've nothing better to do!" declared some Carnforthians.

PARLOUR ENTERTAINMENT

A piano in the parlour was the STATUS SYMBOL of the age - let the Jones's keep up with that! It was the daughter of the family who usually had piano lessons and so provided the music at get-togethers. Men sang or accompanied on the concertina (squeeze-box) or tin whistle. Bones and spoons emphasised the rhythm.

To enhance the light from the lamp on the table, a pair of PRICES DECORATIVE PIANO CANDLES were fixed in the brackets and their gentle glow lit up the popular sheet music of the year:

"THERE WAS I, WAITING AT THE CHURCH", and the beloved tear-jerker, "HOME SWEET HOME".

1907

DOUBLE TRIPS

The wives of some locomotive foot-plate men were quite anxious when their husbands went BOOKING OFF on a DOUBLE TRIP. They didn't know what their men might get up to when they spent the night in railway barracks or lodging, in Carlisle or Crewe for instance. When they read that the Prime Minister had expressed opposition to the CHANNEL TUNNEL BILL, they thought "Good for him"", and heaved sighs of relief for railway wives who lived down south. The very idea of our trains steaming under the English Channel, and defenceless husbands being accommodated in the lodging houses of flighty foreign females gave them palpitations!

A TUNNEL through which Europeans could come and go? NEVER! Far better to build a very high wall to keep them out.

BATHS

In May, the death was reported of a chap called Neil Brodie who was known as the nation's dirtiest man and only bathed when ordered to do so by the Law. Shame on him! Carnforth folk did not need a 'Bobby' to come round and order them to take a bath. They were all very clean in their habits and had a bath every Friday night, whether they needed it or not! On a nail in most back yards hung a large tin bath, ready for action.

BOY SCOUTS

Twenty-five English boys from widely different backgrounds were ferried across Poole Harbour to Brownsea Island to spend a few days in the woods being BOY SCOUTS at an experimental camp, organised by Sir Robert Baden Powell, a hero of the Boer War. The boys were taught woodcraft, fire-making, tracking, life-saving and first aid, and these it was hoped would foster in them a sense of discipline, duty, unselfishness and good citizenship.

Carnforth fathers had a different way of teaching those virtues. They kept their sons very busy weeding the garden, cobbling in the cellar to keep the family shod, chopping firewood, feeding the hens and also delivering orders for tradesmen. Those tired lads would have loved to be camping at Hest Bank, Silverdale or Kellet, and wondered if Carnforth would ever have a troop of Boy Scouts.

HOME REMEDY

When icy winds blew across the PENNINES, there was no need to cough and bark all winter. Doctors' medicines were expensive and nothing like as effective as home-made concoctions. Here is a popular Carnforth Cough Mixture:

Two pennyworth each of LAUDANUM (watch it!), PARAGORIC, ANISEED, PEPPERMINT and HARD SPANISH (liquorice). One pennyworth of TREACLE & WHITE WINE VINEGAR, 4 pennyworth of

HONEY, 2 QUARTS of WATER.

The whole mixture had to be boiled down to one pint. A whole big jugful for 1s 4d!

LOCAL SHOPS

1. W HALES, adjoining the BANK OF LIVERPOOL in Victoria Buildings (lower New Street), was a high-class BESPOKE TAILOR, HATTER & OUTFITTER.

All Carnforth men had to be measured for their suits (trousers, jackets and waistcoats). *[There were no off-the-peg jobs!]*

Mr Hales advertised 'A Trial Respectfully Solicited'. Most Co-operative Society members however preferred to go to the Drapery Department at the top of Market Street to be 'measured-up'.

2. On Scotland Road was the shop of Joseph Walmsley (est. 1866). He was advertised as a PLUMBER, GLAZIER, HOUSE PAINTER and PAPER HANGER. He was a DEALER in LAMPS and LAMP-OIL and promised "PUMPS & WATER CLOSETS NEATLY FITTED-UP".

[These water-closets were certainly needed. Most houses had very smelly EARTH CLOSETS stationed near their back-doors. Haws Hill, however, had more hygienic arrangements, namely Tipper-Buckets at the bottom of a 6ft drop in their backyard conveniences. Water flushed down the back kitchen sink and flowed along an underground pipe into the bucket, which tipped when full. It was highly

probable that a small child, paying a call to one of those horrors, might never be seen again].

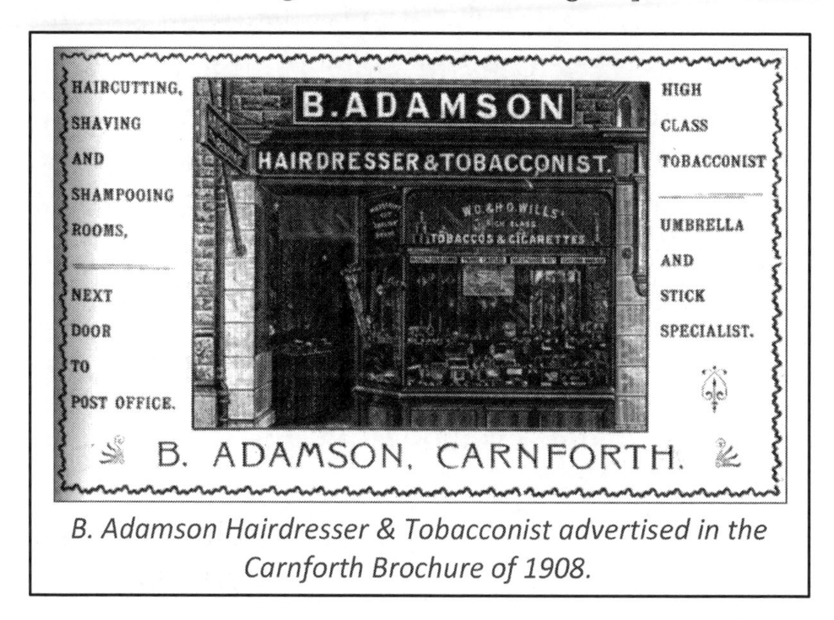

B. Adamson Hairdresser & Tobacconist advertised in the Carnforth Brochure of 1908.

3. Ben Adamson, the Barber, provided an excellent service for men at his shop with the white-and-red striped pole. Carnforth did not have a hairdressing salon for ladies, but there was little need of one. All females wore their hair long. Schoolgirls usually favoured plaits and young ladies fastened back their locks, with wide ribbons tied in a big bow. It was a step towards maturity when a girl PUT UP HER HAIR, either into a BUN on top of her head or at the nape of her neck, firmly anchored with metal hair-pins in the shape of a long narrow U.

EMPIRE DAY

Children at THE NATIONAL SCHOOL enjoyed EMPIRE DAY, which was celebrated on May 24th, the birthday of the late Queen Victoria (God rest her soul!). A teacher played "Land of Hope and Glory", "Rule Britannia" and other patriotic songs on the piano, whilst the children marched smartly around the classrooms, proudly saluting the Union Jack and the large wall-map of the world, with many areas coloured pink to show that they were part of our mighty Empire which occupied one-fifth of the land surface of the globe.

MIGHTY SHIPS

There was keen rivalry among the world powers to see which nation could build the biggest and fastest ocean liner.

In October, Carnforth, with the rest of Britain, rejoiced in the news that our new ship, "THE LUSITANIA", had sailed the passenger route across the Atlantic Ocean to the USA in just 4 days 19 hours and 52 minutes. Thus we had beaten the record of the German liner, "Deutschland", and won the BLUE RIBAND Award. "The Lusitania" had proved that she was the most brilliant ship the world had ever seen, and her captain praised her too. "She's a daisy!" he said.

In November, a group of Carnforth railwaymen used their free passes to go to Liverpool to see Lusitania's sister ship, Cunard's "MAURITANIA", set sail on her maiden voyage to America. They were dismayed to hear, one month later, that she had run aground ... in spite of being bigger and better!

"RACING SHIPS" became a popular street game in Carnforth: exciting, and requiring no expenditure! Passing adults would hear such remarks as, "Bags me the Lusitania", "I hate being that German Deutschland!" and "Oh heck! I'm fed up of being a rotten old French liner again!"

[No one seemed to know the origin of that expression "BAGS ME", but generations of Carnforth children knew exactly what it meant.]

ROYAL RELATIVES

In November, the daily newspapers had many pictures of Kaiser Wilhelm, imperial Emperor of Germany and King of Prussia, who was paying a state visit to his royal relatives in Buckingham Palace. As the two great rulers, our King and the Kaiser, went in a parade to have lunch with the Lord Mayor, the crowds were impressed with the big, strongly-built German, in his magnificent uniform, who was the most powerful military monarch in the world.

After the meal, Kaiser Wilhelm gave a toast: "Blood is thicker than water. May this be so between our countries, Germany and Britain, and may this great city of London develop under the reign of King Edward VII, MY BELOVED UNCLE."

[Carnforth lads had no idea that, within a decade, that resplendent foreign figure would be the cause of their early deaths!]

THE LADY OF THE LAMP

King Edward VII appointed 87-year-old FLORENCE NIGHTINGALE to the Order of Merit. This information may have been of little interest to many Carnforthians, but it greatly impressed William Barnham, whose father, Richard, had fought in the CRIMEAN WAR and so had connections with that famous nurse. Proudly displayed on the living room wall of 39 Highfield Terrace were Richard Barnham's medals, mounted on red velvet in a heavy gilt frame. The family treasured this and the trophies he had brought back from the battlefields, but most interesting of all was the diary he had written as he fought in that ill-fated war and survived terrible scenes of death, disease and disaster.

[It is amazing that this young man, the eldest in a family of 14 children, was able to read and write in that age when a large percentage of the population was illiterate.]

FOOD FOR THOUGHT

A couple of topics had set tongues wagging in the Queen's Hotel in Market Street:

1. Parliament had had the second reading of a Bill which would allow WOMEN to sit in County and Borough Councils.

2. Lloyd George had approved plans for a Channel Ferry Service to sail between Dover and Calais.

[But no Carnforth person would ever be likely to use that!]

THE HIT SONG OF THE YEAR

The best-seller in the sheet music world was that doleful song, "IF THOSE LIPS COULD ONLY SPEAK". (But you're only a beautiful picture in a beautiful gilded frame.)

The Barnham family at the back of 39 Highfield Terrace. Parents were extremely proud of their children and were delighted when a photographer arrived to take a picture which could be put in the Family Album.

1908

CARNFORTH ... HOLIDAY TOWN

Holidays were becoming more popular and Carnforth, realising its potential as a small town set in beautiful surroundings, brought out an illustrated brochure entitled "GUIDE TO CARNFORTH AND DISTRICT . . . THE GATEWAY TO THE WEST COUNTRY." *[This was geographically incorrect! "Railway Centre for the NORTH WEST", it should have claimed.]*

Some young Carnforth men emigrated to the Colonies, none holidayed abroad!

The booklet was edited by J P Porteus, The Pharmacy, 30 Market Street, who took the photographs along with Miss E Barton (sister of Edward Barton, General Manager of the Iron Works). It was published by the CARNFORTH IMPROVEMENT SYNDICATE (Secretary, C Macdonald, Jeweller, Market Street and Treasurer A Hoyle, Station Hotel) and printed by W J WEEKS, Printer and Stationer, 38 Market Street.

C. MacDonald Jewellery Shop advertised in the Carnforth Brochure of 1908.

The holiday-makers would arrive at our busy railway station and, walking out of its impressive façade, they would see our well-designed stone buildings with attractively 'rounded' corners, e.g. the splendid STATION HOTEL, STATION BUILDINGS, HARTLEY'S SHOP at the cross-roads etc., all little over 20 years old and looking very clean and smart.

Rich visitors, who had travelled first class on the train, could afford to stay at the prestigious STATION HOTEL (Proprietor Alfred Hoyle), where they could enjoy every comfort and excellent cuisine. Its horse-drawn carriages could be hired for picnics or pleasant outings to Hornby, Silverdale, the Farleton district etc. Town-dwellers particularly loved the whiff of sea-breezes on rides along the coast to Hest Bank, Morecambe, Bare and Heysham.

Less well-to-do visitors could choose accommodation from the advertised list of apartments and lodgings as follows:

Mrs Forrester, 34 New Street, Sitting-room and 1 bedroom

Mrs Swindlehurt, 41 Bank Terrace, Sitting-room & 1 bedroom

Mrs Metcalfe, 14 Lancaster Road, Sitting-room & 2 bedrooms

Mrs F Kellet, 28 New Street, Sitting-room & 2 bedrooms

Mrs Stretch, 4 Victoria Street, Sitting-room & 2 bedrooms

Mrs Ezra Whinray, Willow Cottage, Sitting-room & 2 bedrooms

Mrs Smith, 17 New Street, Apartments and Boarders and the use of a BATH!

[How was this filled with hot water, I wonder? Was the bath a tiny one near the set-boiler in the back-yard wash-house?]

Braithwaite's, one of the houses near Canal Bridge, advertised TEAS, REFRESHMENTS and Celebrated Gingerbread.

For people who had to be careful about spending money, the town brochure suggested a number of pretty walks to Bolton Brow, Kellet Seeds, Dunnal Mill Caves and by the River Keer.

The Carnforth Cycle Company, now also known as The Motor Company, had left its early premises, in an old white-washed building adjacent to the Carnforth Inn, and moved to a fine new garage in Scotland Road (numbers 5 & 7). That was where visitors went to hire cycles. The holiday Guide Book gave a list of nearby villages to which they might like to travel and by each was the distance from Carnforth in miles e.g.: Arkholme (6½), Beetham (6), Caton (6), Arnside (7), Slyne (4), Kirkby Lonsdale (11), Levens (9), Halton (6).

Anglers were encouraged to come here by the promise that our canal abounded with perch, roach, pike and eels. The River Keer was said to have plenty of trout and, in the latter part of the year, had large runs of salmon, trout and mort. Then there was sea-fishing in the waters of Morecambe Bay.

Carnforth's tradesmen were keen to attract visitors

to their shops.

As few people owned cameras, W. R. TAYLOR, Photographer of 38 Lancaster Rd, invited people to let him provide pictures of themselves to take home as souvenirs. Postcard size photos cost 3s 0d per dozen.

C Macdonald of 25 Market Street advertised his shop most impressively as a FANCY GOODS REPOSITORY. He was a jeweller, watch-maker, gold and silver smith and he sold spectacles, field-glasses, barometers, ladies' vanity dressing bags, umbrellas, gold-mounted walking-sticks etc. As a special memento for holiday-makers, he sold Goss HERALDIC CHINA bearing a crest with 'CARNFORTH' printed below it.

[It would appear that this was merely an advertising gimmick as our town has never had its own crest. Nevertheless my mother bought a tiny cup and was proud to have it on display].

TAYLORS of 38 Lancaster Road, invited people to buy their delicious confectionary and bread, and to "carry away with you pleasant memories of your holiday".

J KNOWLES General House Furnishers advertised upholstered drawing-room suites from £6 6s (a sofa, 2 chairs and an arm-chair), bedroom-suites in satin walnut from £8 8s (bed, wardrobe, dressing table, wash-stand).

J P PORTEUS, The Pharmacy, Market Street, advertised a delightful souvenir from this district: an eye-catching bottle of WARTONIAN Sweet Pea perfume - "A dainty present for your friend" *[Female, we presume].* The attractive label bore the historic Washington Coat of arms, which was said to have suggested the idea of the American Stars and Stripes.

Dr Jackson, local Medical Officer of Health, reported that the death-rate of the district was low, and the longevity of local people proved that the area has a healthy climate, with the pleasant, bracing breezes.

The Carnforth Guide presented our town as the centre of a district of surprising beauty and interest. When, in the mind's eye, a wheel is drawn around it, every 'spoke' leads off to fresh fields of delight.

PENSIONS

In the Budget Debate of May 17th, Mr Asquith, who had become Prime Minister in place of Sir Henry Campbell-Bannerman, announced that the Government intended to introduce an OLD AGE PENSION.

There would be some exceptions:

1. People who had failed to work according to their abilities.

2. Prisoners.

3. The Insane.

4. Paupers.

Note the Modesty Board! National School, Carnforth 1908.
Headmaster: Mr D P Miller.

Back Row: *L Pattinson, J Hunter, A Walmsley, A Jessop, A Thompson, J Greenwood, M Taylor.*
Middle: *F Morris, H Davies, C Byram, D Cape, D Pierce, B Thompson.*
Front: *D Wilkinson, F Howie, M Speight, L Kinder, E Barnes, A Iniff, E Bradley.*

SCHOOL PHOTOGRAPH

Headmaster DAN MILLER and one of his teachers,

MISS LIZZIE HIGH, were photographed with a class of girls in the playground of the NATIONAL SCHOOL. A MODESTY BOARD had been placed in front of the group to conceal the lower legs of the girls. *[Shades of Victorianism!]*

One of the girls, Deborah Wilkinson, became a teacher at the school when she grew up, and her sister Josephine became headmistress of Over Kellet School. The Wilkinson family *[not relatives of mine!]* lived on Kellet Road and their house had a large garden at the back and a pleasant orchard at the side.

CARNFORTH MOTOR (Ex Cycle) COMPANY

The firm was flourishing at its new premises on Scotland Road, and now dealt in motorcars and motorcycles, whilst still doing a brisk trade in selling and hiring-out bicycles.

A late 19th century view down what is now Hawk Street.

Across the road, at the bottom of Hawk Street, GREENLANDS owned another busy garage at around this time. They specialised in the sale of motorcycles, some with side-cars.

EXTENDED FAMILIES

When they grew up and got married, many children chose to rent a house quite near the home of their parents. Carnforth became a town with a lot of extended families. Maybe Grandparents lived up North Road and Mother and Father's address was Alma Terrace. Brother Willi and his family were in Oxford Street and Sister Nellie and her husband lived in King Street. This meant that lot of family visiting went on: "I'll just pop down Hunter Street and see how Auntie Emma and Uncle Aaron are getting on" etc.

King Edward VII and Queen Alexandra also liked family-visiting, but theirs necessitated a trip abroad in many cases.

Queen Victoria's large family had not chosen to take up dwellings around Buckingham Palace. They had married into the Royal Families of several European countries.

In June, our king went to visit his nephew-in-law, CZAR NICHOLAS II of RUSSIA. Off he sailed in the ROYAL YACHT, and those two mighty monarchs, who ruled over the largest empires on earth, met aboard the "Victoria and Albert" when it anchored in the Baltic Sea off the coast of Estonia.

They had BANQUETS and BALLS at their family get-together - NOT a natter over a cup of tea and a jam buttie!

NEWSY TITBITS TO TALK ABOUT

1. Why had that Labour chap, Keir Hardie, not been invited to the ROYAL GARDEN PARTY with the other MPs?

2. It had been suggested at the Trades Union Conference that motors should have a maximum speed limit of 15mph, but wasn't that dangerously high?

3. The PENNY POST to the USA started on October 1st. Was that a good idea?

4. The Admiralty had acquired a new torpedo, with a 4-mile range and a speed of 4 knots. Weren't those a waste of tax-payers' good money?

5. A Botany professor claimed in November that PLANTS HAVE EYES AND CAN SEE . . . did you ever hear the likes of that?

[The Prince of Wales, eldest son Queen Elizabeth II, says that he talks to plants, so he must believe they have ears and can listen. SEEING and HEARING plants will soon be as intelligent as people!]

SING-SONGS OF THE YEAR

"Shine of Harvest Moon" and "Oh! Oh! Antonio" (about a soppy girl who had fallen in love with an

Italian ice-cream vender).

[He was never seen round Carnforth streets!]

1909

OLD AGE PENSIONS

January 1st was a Happy New Year's Day for Carnforth's 70 year-olds (and above) and a very busy day for our Post Office at the far end of Station Buildings, near the bridge over the main railway line. Our old 'uns toddled along to draw the State's first OLD AGE PENSION - 5 shillings for one person and 7s 6d for a married couple.

The Post Office in Station Buildings viewed from the bridge over the main railway line. Note Station Hotel's main entrance on the corner, and the huge name hoarding on the roof.

Of course, they did not expect to live on the money!

Throughout their lives, they had been careful to live within their means, and had striven to save at least a few coppers each week to provide a NEST-EGG for their old age. The new pension would provide them with a few delightful extras.

It was concluded, at the end of the day, that claimants all over the country had been extremely polite and patient, and most had looked very neat. They had shown delight that the payments were not like POOR RELIEF, but pensions such as those paid by the state to soldiers and sailors.

TAXES

Lloyd George, the Chancellor of the Exchequer, brought in his PEOPLE'S BUDGET in April. It was said to be the most radical one in our nation's history. Money had to be raised to pay out Old Age Pensions and to finance the Navy, which was getting 6 more DREADNOUGHTS in the re-armament programme. Taxation was to be higher - the 100,000 people with incomes over £5000 per annum would pay a new Super Tax of 6d in the £. The standard rate of tax on earned income would remain at 9d up to £2000 per annum, and one shilling over that level. There would also be higher taxation on alcohol, tobacco and petrol.

Carnforth working-men did not worry about income tax rises. They would not be paying any, because they mostly earned only £50 - £100 per annum.

THE SALVATION ARMY

The local corps was proud to learn that some of its collection money was helping to ease a grave problem in the London Territory.

Homeless and unemployed down-and-outs were congregating on the Thames Embankment and making it a very unpleasant place. Their only chance of food and shelter was from the Salvation Army, who fed as many as 640 vagrants each night and provided shelter for some during the early hours of the morning.

HEROES

Carnforth boys aged 13+, who went by train each day to attend THE TECHNICAL SCHOOL ('Tec' for short) in the STOREY'S INSTITUTE near the railway station and castle in LANCASTER, had a new aviation hero: a Frenchman named Louis Bleriot, who was the first person to fly across the Channel in an aeroplane. The flight from Calais to Dover Castle, a distance of 31 miles, had taken 43 minutes, at a speed of 40mph. This exploit won Bleriot a prize of £1000 awarded by the Daily Mail.

Another hero at 'THE TEC' was the scientist MARCONI, an Italian who won the Nobel Prize in Physics for his contribution to the development of WIRELESS. Some lads longed to be electricians.

CHRIST CHURCH

The congregation of the Parish Church was working hard to raise money for important alterations to the building. Their aim was to have a TOWER erected with BELLS and a CLOCK, which could give the church an impressive appearance.

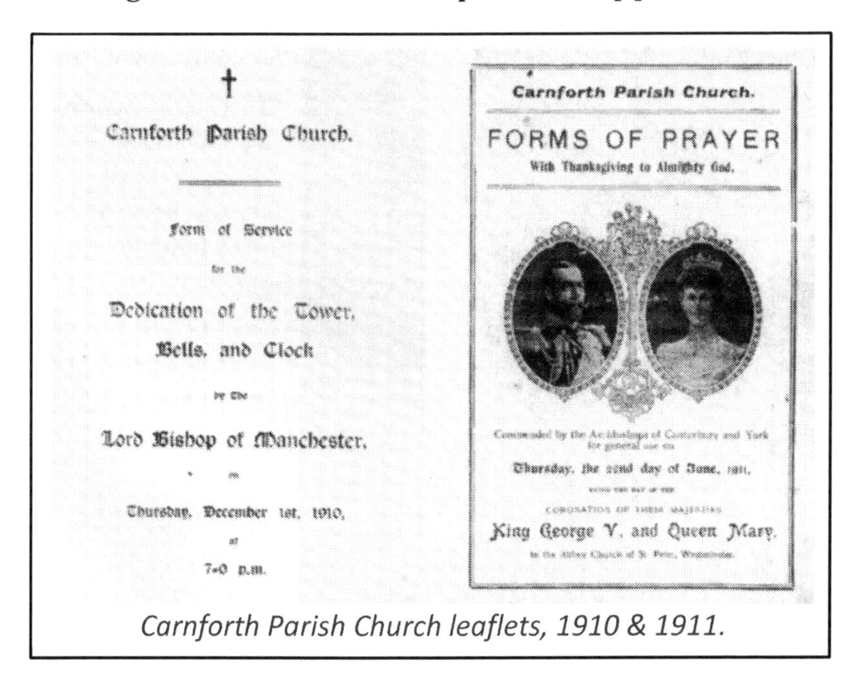

Carnforth Parish Church.

Form of Service

Dedication of the Tower,
Bells, and Clock

Lord Bishop of Manchester,

Thursday, December 1st, 1910,

7-0 p.m.

Carnforth Parish Church.

FORMS OF PRAYER
With Thanksgiving to Almighty God.

Thursday, the 22nd day of June, 1911,

King George V. and Queen Mary.

Carnforth Parish Church leaflets, 1910 & 1911.

One successful fund-raiser was the sale of a COOKERY BOOK, people having paid to have their favourite recipes included. Mr Bibby, the bank manager, had submitted a recipe for a BACHELOR CAKE. Other 'famous' contributors were Miss Jackson (Hall Gowan), Mrs Dockray (Seed Merchant's firm), Mrs Baty (Co-op General Manager's wife), Mrs High (School teacher's mother), Mrs Carr (of the famous TOFFEE SHOP), Mrs Slinger (farmer's wife), Mrs Wrightson (from the Nurseries), Mrs Whinray (Joiner's wife).

BARLEY WATER RECIPE

1. Boil ½lb pearl barley in 5 quarts water for 20 mins.

2. Strain through muslin.

3. Add 6 lemons and ½lb Demerara sugar.

4. Stand to cool.

A PICK-ME-UP

Juice of 4 lemons and rind of 2.

Add 1lb sugar.

Pour on 1 quart boiling water. Cool. Strain.

Add 6 beaten egg yolks and 1 gill of CREAM. Mix.

Put into a gallon bottle.

Add 1 BOTTLE OF SHERRY.

Take a wine-glassful 3 times daily (yes! yes!)

SHOPPING

Newspapers reported that a firm called SELFRIDGES had opened a new store in London's Oxford Street on March 15th - 6 acres of departments, lounges, restaurants and a bargain basement.

Carnforth women were not unduly impressed. Our Oxford Street had no shops, but everything a body might need could be bought at our fine specialist shops in Market Street, New Street and along stretches of Lancaster and Scotland Roads.

G. Rathbone's Music Shop, 2 & 4 New Street. Note the street's smart, two-toned brickwork and the coloured tile border under the eaves.

The fragrant aroma of freshly-ground coffee wafted from HIMSWORTH'S GROCERY SHOP, 4 New Street, Tea and Coffee Specialists and Purveyors of High Class Provisions. Prices ranged from 1s 6d to 2s 6d per lb (7½ to 12½p). Their coffee, roasted frequently and ground as required for each customer, cost 1s 8d per lb. Mixed with a little chicory, it only cost 1s 0d per lb. They bought only the finest provisions and guaranteed absolute cleanliness in handling them. Homemade bread was a speciality.

The HIMSWORTHS were keen members of the

Congregational Church. Mr Himsworth had a severe speech impediment, but was an excellent singer with the choir.

"BOOTS, BOOTS, BOOTS" *[Not the famous Chemist shop].* F W LAMBERT'S (17 Market Street) was the leading and oldest-established boot shop in town. He sold registered brands of the best boots, and specialised in boot repairing, using only the good English leather.

Men, women and children all wore boots (or clogs). Lightweight boots for ladies were fastened with small, spherical shoe-buttons, which needed BUTTON HOOKS to guide them through the holes.

[Apparently this shop did NOT sell shoes, but in cities and large towns LADIES OF FASHION were wearing lace-up shoes, made of patent leather or glacé kid with shaped high heels and cost around 9s 11d - about half a working man's wage!]

THE CO-OP v HARTLEY'S

There was keen rivalry for custom between Carnforth's two biggest grocers. HARTLEY'S had the reputation for being our area's best caterers, having first started the trade here in 1863, when they had supplied food for the 'navvies' who were building our local railways. Carnforth then had less than 400 inhabitants and no shops of any size.

Co-operative Wholesale Societies were prospering all over Britain, because members liked the idea of the ‘Co-op’ *[pronounced Cwop or Cope]* taking care of many aspects of their lives. Besides retailing goods of all varieties, it took charge of insurance, banking, catering, funeral arrangements, educational classes and had a Cottage Fund to buy houses for members, who repaid the money as weekly rental.

Top: *Hartley’s shop at Millhead, over the Keer bridge.*
Centre: *Our River.*
Bottom: *Warton, where Carnforthians were buried.*

In New Street, Carnforth Society had 4 adjacent

shops (footwear, grocery, butchery, bakery and confectionary) under the splendid Co-op Hall and the office with an adjoining Board Room. These premises had been opened in 1888.

The Society also had 2 busy shops at the top of Market Street:

1. A large furnishing and hardware department.

2. A drapery and clothing shop (suits made to measure for ladies and gentlemen).

Both HARTLEY'S (at the Carnforth Inn crossroads) and our Co-op had efficient DELIVERY SERVICES, by horse-and-cart, to the homes of their customers.

PAINTING AND DECORATING

Thomas Rathbone of Hawk Street and J Walmsley of Scotland Road (also a Plumber) advertised as Painters and Decorators.

Only people who were fairly well-to-do would be able to afford their services. Working-class folk did their own decorating – 'white-washing' the back kitchen with a mixture of 'quick' lime and water, distempering the living room and bedrooms perhaps, and wallpapering the parlour.

Family groups frequently shared a large trestle-table, which they passed from one to the other at Spring-cleaning time. Using large, flat brushes, they coated the back of wallpaper with a gooey paste made from flour and hot water, which had to be carefully mixed to avoid lumps.

Mr Rathbone was an artistic man who specialised in sign-writing. He was also a choir master and a photographer.

INGHAM & CO: 38 MARKET STREET

This shop sold presents of every description, local crested china, postcards and framed pictures of the district, games, baskets, and all the latest novelties in toys. It also stocked a mouth-watering selection of sweets and rock, and had fresh fruit daily.

[W J Weeks, the Printer, also advertised 38 Market Street as his business address so it would seem that the premises were shared, Mr Weeks having his printing press in the cellar. When Ingham's closed down, it is surmised that the Visitor (local Morecambe newspaper) took over the shop and rented it to Mr Weeks, who then ran it as a newsagent's. Later he owned the premises.]

THE WHINRAYS

Edward Whinray was advertised as a Complete House Furnisher at 5 Market Street. The firm had been established over 30 years. Ezra Whinray (his brother) of Haws Hill and Lancaster Road was a joiner and undertaker.

[I remember him as an old man who muttered streams of swear words at himself as he quietly did joinery jobs. He made me a rolling-pin as a wedding-present in 1940 and I still use it today.]

BUTCHER BILLY

"Williams" had been a popular butcher's shop in Market Street since 1872. The father should have given the matter a little thought before naming his son WILLIAM (William Williams!)

The firm had a slaughter house alongside Scotland Road.

A WIFE FOR POPEYE THE SAILOR MAN

Alfred Hoyle, Wine and Spirit Merchant, who was the proprietor of the Station Hotel, had a son who married Miss Olive Stodd of Hill Street She thus became Olive Oil. *[Carnforthians didn't bother to sound the letter H.]*

WORK-HOUSES

The dread of very poor Carnforth families was that they would not be able to pay their way and would end up in that dreadful place, THE WORKHOUSE, a grim grey building near Williamson Park in Lancaster. This meant a constant fight against poverty by practising THRIFT and getting value for every farthing.

People in desperate need could apply to a BOARD OF GUARDIANS for a little financial aid. The Government had now decided to scrap the Boards and pass on their power to counties and country boroughs. Only unemployed people of good character would be given help.

SUFFERING SUFFRAGETTES

In September, women, waiting their turn to be served with margarine, cheese or bacon at the marble-topped counter in our Co-op Grocery Department, were loud in their condemnation of cruelty being inflicted on suffragettes in jail. Nine had been imprisoned, and had continued their battle to gain 'VOTES FOR WOMEN' by going on hunger strike. The upsetting news was that they were being force-fed.

One woman had a tube inserted up her nose when a feeding-cup could not be forced between her teeth, and because of a previous nasal injury she had been made ill and was hospitalised.

Up till now, the suffragettes had had little support from the public, but they did gain some sympathy at this time. It was felt that force-feeding them was unacceptable treatment.

A RATTLER

FORDS introduced the first mass-produced car, the MODEL T, which was to become famous as the "TIN LIZZIE". Henry Ford said it could be bought in ANY colour, as long as it was BLACK. The price was said to be within the range of most people.

So far the Carnforth Motor Company had only dealt with 'handmade' cars. It was hoped the new model would boost local trade.

TOPICS FOR THE TOP CLASSES

1. Children at the National School (Lancaster Road) and British School (off Hawk Street) were proud to learn that Shakleton, the Explorer, had got the closest ever to the South Pole. At the magnetic pole, he planted a Union Jack which had been given to him by Queen Victoria.

2. None had been seen in Carnforth yet, but a promising new material had made its appearance: BAKELITE - light, strong and wouldn't corrode.

3. The King had opened a marvellous museum in London. It was named "THE VICTORIA AND ALBERT".

4. In March, the First International Exhibition of AIR-CRAFT was opened. The most expensive model cost £1,440.

A POINT FOR MOTHERS TO PONDER

In a New Street backyard, Mrs So-and-so 'mother of 8' was sweating as she vigorously dollied a tubful of washing. She felt very annoyed when she thought of the Government edict: "A WIFE IS NOT ENTITLED TO A DIVORCE, EVEN IF HER HUSBAND HAS DESERTED HER."

(Cheers for the Suffragettes! We're on their side now. It's time we women had some rights).

HAS ANYONE SEEN HIM?

As they went on their around our streets, errand-boys were heard whistling the new popular song, "HAS ANYONE HERE SEEN KELLY?"

No one had. Probably he couldn't afford the cost of the sea fare from the Isle of Man.

1910

Work was going ahead to build the TOWER proposed for the Parish Church extension. It was planned that it would be 50ft high and crowned with a 20ft spirette, pointing heavenward. The construction, along with a clock, would cost £1,100. There would be an additional cost of £220 for a belfry with a wonderful peal of tubular bells.

My mother and her young friends were among the congregation who felt inspired to improve the rather plain church and to give it a more impressive, dignified appearance. To raise money, everyone was working very hard by holding whist drives, bazaars, sales-of-work, concerts, tea parties, and conversaziones in the Church Room (Preston St.) The sale of the RECIPE BOOK continued to bring in money, and well-known tradespeople were willing to advertise in it e.g. G W Collinge of Market Street, Ironmonger, had cruets for sale at 4s 6d (22½p), photo frames from 8d - 6s 6d (3½ - 32½p) and incandescent mantels for gas-lights at 4d.

ROYAL DEATH

On May 6th, Carnforth shared in our country's sadness at the news of the death of our Most Gracious Sovereign-Lord, King Edward VII. He had died of pneumonia.

At his funeral, his nephew, Kaiser Wilhelm of Germany, was extremely annoyed at having to give precedence to a DOG! Led by a servant, King Edward's fox-terrier, called Caesar, was given pride of place behind the coffin.

Next in the procession came our new King George V and his wife Queen Mary.

CARNFORTH SORROW

A memorial service for the late King Edward was held in our Parish Church at 1pm on May 20th. A leaflet giving the order of service was printed W J Weeks, 38 Market Street. The hymns sung at the service were, "O God our Help in Ages Past", "Now the Labourers' Task is O'er" and "Brief Life is Here our Portion", followed by the "Dead March".

As usual, Carnforth's patriotic citizens kept their leaflets as one more souvenir of a very auspicious occasion.

MURDER MOST FOUL!

Murders never seemed to happen around here, so Carnforthians tended to find national newspaper reports about them very enthralling. A mystery was recorded in July. The wife of an American doctor, H H CRIPPEN by name, had disappeared from her London home. A few days later he too disappeared and then the mutilated, dismembered remains of his wife were dug from their cellar floor.

Anxious to keep up with the gory tale as it unrolled, people watched for the arrival of their 'dailies' each morning. The exciting climax to the mystery took place on board a ship from Belgium as it neared the coast of Canada. Dr Crippen, accompanied by his young mistress, was charged with the brutal murder of his wife, and became the first criminal in the world to be caught by RADIO.

FLORENCE NIGHTINGALE

William Barnham was sad in August when he read of the funeral of Florence Nightingale, the FOUNDER OF NURSING.

On her coffin was a huge, white floral cross from the matrons and nurses of all London Hospitals. There was a wreath shaped like an army lantern of the type she had carried on her rounds in Scutari Hospital during the Crimean War, and a cushion of flowers which had been sent by survivors of the Charge of the Light Brigade.

William's father, Richard Barnham, had fought at THE ALMA, INKERMAN and SEBASTOPOL but as a rifleman, not as a solider in a Cavalry Regiment.

[Carnforth's ALMA TERRCE {now Upper Market St.} was named as a reminder of the Crimean victory and quite a number of baby girls were christened Alma.]

THE MOVIES

D W Griffith's film, "In Old California", went on release to cinemas. It had been made at a place which no one in Carnforth had ever heard of: HOLLYWOOD, near Los Angeles in America.

There was no cinema here to show 'MOVING PICTURES', but some people were determined that we WOULD have one - someday!

FUTURE GIRL GUIDES

Miss Lambert and Miss Rawbotham were teachers at the BRITISH SCHOOL (Headmaster Mr R T Barnard). They told their girl pupils about Agnes Baden-Powell (sister of Sir Robert) who was starting up the GIRL GUIDE MOVEMENT, which encouraged obedience, clean-living and resourcefulness. The scholars hoped they would be able to join when Carnforth got a company.

RAMSAY'S BLOUSE FACTORY

The chugging of the busy engine at Ramsay's Mill in Rigg's Yard could be heard all around the Hill Street, Stanley Street, Lancaster Road and Oxford Street areas. It drove the sewing machines, which raced along at an alarming speed. The workers liked that because they were on PIECE-WORK - the more garments they completed, the more money they were paid. Sadly, only a few coppers per dozen *[Sweated labour we would call it today!]*

Those zooming machines could be really dangerous. Sometimes a girl would be seen slumped over her sewing. She had been distracted for a moment, and the needle had pierced one of her fingers. The machine had to be switched off before the fainting girl could be released. A piece of scrap material had to be hastily grabbed from a basket-skip to stem the flow of blood, because it would have been dreadful to stain the garment she was making.

My mother, aged 22, had done well as a machinist and eventually became a forewoman. She was pleased when her duties took her out of the noisy mill and away by train to Ramsay's central works, in Kendal, to act as their SICK VISITOR. The visits were not so much concerned about the welfare of the workers there, but to check that their absence was genuinely due to illness - in other words, to make sure they were not 'swinging the lead'. It was better that the Sick Visitor should not be known by the Kendal employees.

HORSES

People argued that what the newspapers printed was not always believable. For instance, it was reported in July that there was a shortage of horses in England. HORSES? Carnforth had horses galore! They were clip-clopping up and down all our streets.

They pulled the town's ambulance, the fire-engine, hearses for funerals, coaches for weddings and carts of all sorts for farmers selling milk and tradespeople selling groceries, fruit & vegetables, hardware, coal, etc. Well-to-do people had governess carts, traps and dog-carts to get them around. Every farm in the area had a team of fine horses and all the boats to-ing and fro-ing on the canal banks were towed by the noble beasts.

Reports stated, however, that our country could face a serious shortage of horses should war break out. 170,000 would be needed immediately and the same number replaced every 6 months. Despite this, Britain was exporting more horses than any other country. Germany and Austria spent £200,000 each annually on horse-breeding, but Britain spent less than £5,000.

In that case, Carnforthians decided that our Government would have to do something about the matter.

SIGHT AT NIGHT

After dark on May 20th, many of our townspeople were out-of-doors, gazing skywards in search of a spectacular object among the stars. Halley's COMET was passing within 13 million miles of earth.

A RAILWAY JOURNEY CARNFORTH STATION

Young Ella, clutching her cardboard suitcase, joined the long queue at the little window of the ticket office in the entrance to Carnforth's busy station.

A cheerful collector snipped the ticket she had bought for Leeds (where her relatives lived) and a smiling porter approached to take her case on his small, two-wheeled truck. As he walked with her along platform 1, an L.N.W.R. express train, speeding from Scotland to London, roared past amid a cloud of steam and smoke, and its ear-splitting whistle made the people on the platform step back hurriedly.

Staff at the southern end of Platform 1. Bays 1 and 2 on extreme right. Number 2 signal box & clock tower on the left.

Before going down the subway, Ella waved to a friend who was about to board a local train for Lancaster, which was standing in Bay 2 on her left. Bay 1 was empty.

Climbing up the incline to Platforms 2 and 3, she noted, by the big station clock, that she had 10 mins to spare, so she stopped at the WHSMITH bookstall facing ahead, read the row of standing boards which head-lined the day's news and chose a magazine to read on her journey.

She then followed her porter as he wove his way

among the crowd waiting for the arrival of the FURNESS LINE train from Barrow at platform 3: ladies with prams, men with bicycles, people going in and out of the refreshment room, porters pulling big trucks laden with parcels, and children jumping around impatient to be on their journeys.

On the right, Ella's train was ready to depart from Bay 3, which was used by the MIDLAND RAILWAY COMPANY. The helpful porter opened the door of a 3rd class "LADIES ONLY" compartment and, having settled her into a corner window-seat, he heaved her case up on to the luggage-rack, made of strong woven string. He tipped his peak cap and smiled gratefully as she slipped a silver 3d bit into his hand for his kindness.

Carnforth L.N.W.R. Station. Later picture, Platforms 2 & 3. W.H.Smith's Newsagents stall in the centre background.

From his van at the end of the train, the guard blew his whistle to alert people nearby, waved his green flag to the driver on the foot-plate to signal that all doors were closed and everything ready for the off. With a noisy hiss of steam and some energetic chuffs and puffs from the engine, the train for Leeds pulled out of Carnforth Station when the signal moved to the down position and shone green for "GO".

THE JOURNEY

The train crossed the bridge over Warton Road and gathered speed as it passed the East Junction Signal-box and Netherbeck. Ella consulted politely with her travelling companions to ensure that conditions were right for a comfortable journey: the window-blinds partly pulled down to shield their eyes from bright sunlight; the brass handle of the heating-regulator turned to OFF so that no hot air from under the seats would cause their ankles to swell; the windows in the two doors fixed half-open to allow a current of cool air to circulate around the compartment. (A window was opened and closed by means of a broad leather strap with holes along its length, which could be hooked on to a small knob on the door).

The facing seats, upholstered in strong-wearing material, were each designed to accommodate 6 passengers, and above them was a row of pictures featuring famous beauty-spots. The views of Yorkshire seen from the train could rival any of them, and Ella sat back in her seat and enjoyed the journey as telegraph poles flashed by her window.

At intervals, the train pulled up at small stations where passengers got off and on, and there was the noisy clatter of milk churns being loaded into the guard's van. BORWICK, ARKHOLME, MELLING (with its long dark tunnel), WENNINGTON (where the stretch off line from Carnforth was connected with the LANCASTER to LEEDS MIDLAND RAILWAY IN 1866), BENTHAM, CLAPHAM and the village with the delightful name, GIGGLESWICK, LONG PRESTON, and then the bigger, busier stations: HELLIFIELD, SKIPTON, KEIGHLEY, and finally the important destination, LEEDS.

The correct outline for a railway engine! My father Tom (bottom left) and Joe Atack (top right) posing proudly on their locomotive outside the L.N.W.R. Shed.

Along the top of each compartment was an EMERGENCY CORD, with the threatening notice beside it: "PENALTY FOR IMPROPER USE £5". There were very few occasions when these cords were pulled, but emergencies of a certain kind frequently occurred on this journey, which took almost 3 hours in the unconnected compartments.

[Modern facilities such as corridors, toilets and buffet coaches had not been introduced!]

If a passenger had an urgent need for a toilet, he had to jump off at a station, ask the guard, "Please may I leave the train?", and dash into a waiting-room, which hopefully had a lavatory. Only MALE passengers did that! Modest ladies sat with legs crossed tightly!

(1st and 2nd class compartments were more roomy and comfortable, and the seats had arm-rests and crocheted antimacassars with the monogram of the railway company worked in them.)

A RAILWAY JOURNEY WAS AN EXCITING EXPERIENCE.

LABOUR EXCHANGES

Under a Government Act, the first ever LABOUR EXCHANGES were opened - 80 of them throughout the country. It was reported that they were inundated with job-seekers.

Carnforth had had something similar for many years. A lady living in Kellet Road ran an agency, at her private address, for anyone wishing to go into 'service' as a farm or domestic servant.

AN IMPORTANT EVENT

CHRIST CHURCH TOWER with its CLOCK was completed, and Carnforth men could now check their pocket-watches as they passed by. The bells had been safely lifted up within the steeple and, on Thursday December 1st at 7pm, there was a DEDICATION SERVICE OF THE TOWER, BELLS AND CLOCK, led by the Lord Bishop of Manchester.

This was the first year that our town was able to herald in Christmas with the merry ringing of Church Bells.

1911

HAPPY NEW YEAR!

For the first time in Carnforth, the NEW YEAR was welcome in as the Parish Church clock chimed the midnight hour, and joined in with the shrill whistles of all the locomotives in the railway yards, and the cheers of the crowd assembled on the Market Ground.

THE CENSUS

At the beginning of the century Carnforth's population had numbered 3040.

At the census of 1911 it was recorded as 3142, an increase of only 102 over the 10-year period. The town's rapid growth in the second half of the 19th century had halted, and no new streets were being built.

Trade at the Iron Works had become spasmodic with only some of the 6 blast-furnaces working at any one time. Men became redundant, and in search of alternative employment they turned to the railways which, fortunately, were flourishing. More and more people were travelling about and the IRON HORSE reigned supreme in the field of transport.

SHOP WORKERS

Folk from the surrounding villages came to Carnforth by train to buy at our shops, and trade prospered. Unfortunately some employees became worn out through working very long hours, and they were relieved to hear that Winston Churchill had spoken up for their rights in Parliament.

He had stated that the cause Shop Act of 1904 had failed to deal with the social evil caused by assistants having to work 80-90 hours a week. It was proposed that a new Act should be brought in limiting shop workers to a 60 hour week, and the Government should stir-up local authorities to introduce half-day closing times.

REPORT ON CARNFORTH

From **BULMERS HISTORY AND DIRECTORY OF LANCASTER AND DISTRICT 1911**

SCHOOLS

1. The ENDOWED SCHOOL (built in 1851) became THE NATIONAL SCHOOL and is now called THE CHURCH OF ENGLAND SCHOOL.

2. THE BRITISH SCHOOL (off Hawk Street.)

HOTELS

Near the busy and important station is a very fine hotel attached to which is the VICTORIA HALL which holds 200 people and is used for public BALLS, BANQUETS, DINNERS etc. There is also a SKATING RINK.

The QUEEN'S is another good hotel.

Annie Barnham (my mother) around 1900, with her class in playground of National School. Headmaster Dan Miller, Teacher Lizzie High.

There is also the CARNFORTH INN, an ancient hostelry first erected in 1620 and rebuilt in 1904.

<u>THE PRINCIPAL LANDOWNERS IN 1911</u>

William Sharp (J P) of Bleasdale House, Silverdale

William Farrer (D Litt), Hall Garth, Over Kellet

H J Coulston, "Hawkshead", Bolton-le-Sands

John Lee Booker, Esq

Thomas F Jackson, "Meresbeck", Carnforth

Lancelot Jackson, Netherbeck, Carnforth

Miss Erving, Cragbank (daughter of James Erving)

The Miller Family, "Plane Tree House", Carnforth

And Resident Yeomen

SPORTS

Cricket and Bowling Club

POLITICS

Conservative Club

Liberal Club

CLUBS

Oddfellows

Sons of Temperance Rechabites

AMENITIES

Fire Brigade Station

Fever Hospital

Police Station

Auction Mart

Choral Society

National Telephone Call Office: Operator - S Nixon, 18 Lancaster Road

CHURCHES

Christ Church

Wesleyan Chapel

Congregational Church

Carnforth Mission (Rev Harrison)

Salvation Army Barracks (Captain William Baird)

PUBLIC HALLS

1. Co-operative Hall (300 people) New Street

2. Victoria Hall (200 people) Station Hotel

3. Public Hall, Kellet Road

TRANSPORT

Newspapers reported that, in London, HORSE-DRAWN OMNIBUSES were being replaced by MOTOR BUSES.

"I don't want to know that!" said a Carnforthian. "We have neither! It's the train or SHANKS'S PONY for us."

Leeds & Bradford had their first electric trolley-buses and William Barnham was thrilled to ride on one when he visited his relations in Leeds.

Many of our railwaymen enjoyed going for a day's excursion to Blackpool, using their free passes and, from there, some loved the excitement of riding on a trolley along the breezy coast to Fleetwood.

HEATED MATTERS

In July and August, England suffered a terrific heat wave. In London, temperatures reached 97 degrees in the shade. It was the hottest long spell for 70 years and, every week, hundreds of people were dying.

The heat inside Ramsay's Sewing Mill was unbearable, and the girls grumbled and groaned as they sweated over their machines. In all kinds of ways, their working conditions were not as they would have liked them. All those families working very hard for one firm, AND NOT A VOTE AMONG THEM! Women had no say in the running of our country; surely that couldn't be right?

Inside Morphy's Sewing Mill where the girls were on 'piece work'. My mother, Annie, had been made a forewoman. In 1911 the firm employed 140.

The 'Mill Lasses' would have been willing to join in a huge march of between 40,000 and 60,000 in London, all demanding VOTES FOR WOMEN. They were from all over Britain and overseas - women of all classes and walks of life, some dressed as famous females: Boadicea, Joan of Arc and even Queen Victoria. The march ended in an enthusiastic meeting in the Albert Hall.

STRIKES

Some Carnforth men, as well as women, were disgruntled about their working conditions in the quarries, on the railway and at the Iron Works. As far as is known, however, no strikes were held here at this time but, throughout Britain, there was a great deal of dissension, particularly among miners, dockers and textile workers. Some strikes became so violent that troops were used to quell them and some deaths occurred.

It was decided that an Industrial Council would be set up to settle any future disputes. Carnforth workers were pleased about that!

PUNISHMENT

Headmaster Dan Miller and R T Barnard believed in corporal punishment and were very strict disciplinarians. A swishing cane would quickly bring down stinging lashes on the hands (and seat!) of any child, for lateness etc. Scholars were so afraid that they dare not cause trouble. They read with interest newspaper stories about the

Duke of Marlborough, who expressed his support for the use of the birch, and regretted that it might no longer be allowed in his old school or any other public school.

"I'm all for birching", he said. "It's better than writing out lines." Another earl agreed with him, and said that writing out lines could hurt the eyes and be far more harmful than corporal correction.

Our two headmasters didn't consider 'lines' as an alternative to a good dose of the cane. Large classes HAD to be kept in order.

NEW BOSSES

Ramsay's Sewing Mill was sold to the MORPHY family. Improvements were made and new buildings erected.

EVENTS TO NOTE

Most Carnforthians were true patriots and loved to discuss the 'goings-on' of the Royal Family. Topical titbits were:

1. King George V and his visiting German cousin Kaiser Wilhelm II reasserted mutual friendship.

2. The King's eldest son, Prince Edward, was made PRINCE OF WALES at his investiture in Caernarfon Castle.

3. The King unveiled the Queen Victoria Memorial in front of Buckingham Palace.

4. The King and Queen opened the 'FESTIVAL OF EMPIRE' at Crystal Palace.

5. News items of a political nature could cause heated arguments at local meetings. For instance, what were that lot in Westminster getting up to? The Budget proposed paying MPs A SALARY of around £400 per annum. Talk about feathering their own nests!

6. Members of our Conservative and Liberal Clubs were not pleased to note that the Labour Party was growing, and James Ramsay MacDonald had succeeded Keir Hardie as Chairman.

7. Everyone was proud of technical progress in our country and applauded the news that an aeroplane had flown the first AIR MAIL from Hendon to Windsor. Winged letters!

THE CORONATION

The highlight of the year was the coronation of King George V and Queen Mary on June 23rd, amid wonderful scenes of pageantry at Westminster Abbey, which had been transformed with new vivid blue carpeting and banks of beautiful flowers.

During one part of the ceremony, which lasted 7 hours, a golden canopy was held over the king by 4 noblemen. He was given a formidable list of titles:

King of the United Kingdom, Emperor of India, Defender of the Faith, and King of British Dominions beyond the seas.

Carnforth was bedecked with Union Jacks and red, white and blue bunting for the great occasion, and a large congregation assembled in the Parish Church to give thanks to Almighty God. The Archbishops of Canterbury and York had commended a FORM OF PRAYER to be used in churches throughout the land, and leaflets were given to worshippers to follow the Order of Service. These were not printed by Weeks or Smiths of Market Street but by the Advertiser Steam Printing Works of Ormskirk. "O King of Kings whose reign is old" was one of the hymns.

In the afternoon, as at all great occasions, the celebratory processions set off from the Market Ground, proudly led by our 2 excellent bands: the town's Brass Band and the large Salvation Army Band. Fancy Dress competitions, Sporting Events and Teas were enjoyed on the field up North Road.

The century had only moved on 11 years, but our country had had 3 sovereigns.

CARNFORTH TWANG

People who had settled here up to 40 years earlier were still using the dialects of their birthplaces but, from their neighbours and colleagues, had added words from other dialects which they found expressive and to their liking. Thus Carnforth's own unique twang had developed.

Folk of Lancashire descent were THEE-ING and THOU-ING. ("Did THOU lose thy 'at?")

Incomers from Yorkshire still persisted in the ungrammatical use of the verb 'to be'. ("We WAS in us Sund'y best," and "I WERE just off tut shop.")

One young lady, born in Derbyshire, always spoke as though she and her body were separate beings. ("I think I'll wash me", and "I'll just sit me down".)

People born in Cumberland, especially from those around Carlisle, had their own version of the word OUR. ("We've 'ad WURR dinners", and to them rain puddles were DUBS.)

To people from other areas of Britain, some of Carnforth's sayings would need an explanation:

1. "WOTS TER BIN UPTA RAKING OUT THEE-ER TILL NOW?" (This had no connection with gardening. It was a question demanded of young people arriving home late at night.)

2. "COME ON, GERR A-GATE!" (This was not a request for a backyard entrance. It meant, "Get a move on!")

3. "WILTER SIDE YON TABLE?" (A request to remove pots, NOT the furniture)

4. "SHAPE THISELL MI LASS!" *[I would if I could!]*

5. "SLING THY 'OOK!" (This was not a harvest-time instruction. It meant CLEAR OFF!)

6. "YON TWO'S LIVIN OVVER T'BRUSH!" (This translates as, "That couple aren't legally married!")

7. "THOU'S BIN CLOCKING NEX' DOO-ER AGEN!" (No connection with a broody hen. It was said by an accusing husband whose wife had been gossiping at a neighbour's house for a long time.)

8. "WOTS THOU GAWPING AT? IT'S NORR A PIPPY SHOW!" (This meant that it is rude to stare. It may have derived from 'a puppet-show.')

9. "YON KID ALLUS 'AS CANDLES" (pronounced cannels) That child always needs his nose wiping!

10. "HE'S NOBBUT AD A CAT-LICK" (The fellow has not washed himself properly. In fact he has left tide marks!)

11. "MUCKY MURY 'AS CRACKIES AND WICKUNS!" (Dirty Mary has small game in her hair - some in egg form and some alive, with active legs.)

12. "LIL WILLIE'S ALLUS POKING' FER JACKIES" (Small William enjoys nasal excavations)

13. "I'S OFF TUT PETTY" (The back-yard convenience. The Norman word PETTY meant a small building.)

14. "IT WUR SOUR AS WIZZ" (A description of father's rhubarb.)

15. "THOU'LL COP IT, I'LL TELL THI!" (You have trouble ahead!)

16. "TEK A GANDER AT THIS." (Nothing to do with a goose's husband! This meant, "Take a look".)

SOME LOCAL ADJECTIVES:

A COBBED woman - a peculiar one

A LISH chap - a sprightly one

CLARTY ginger bread - deliciously sticky

A PASTEY face - of pale complexion

A KYSTEY child - likes NO offered food

A CRABBY teacher - bad-tempered

A SLONKY female - lazy, sloppy

A GAWMLESS kid - not at all bright!

WALLA (wallow) food - tasteless, lacking salt

A MARDY lass - pampers herself

A FEW VERBS:

To SKEN - stare rudely

To LIG - lie down

To LOLL - lean lazily

To SNITCH - tell tales

To CHUNNER - grumble quietly

To MEE-MOW - mouth words silently

To SHIG - win ALL your friend's marbles

MALARKING & SHINANICKING - playing boisterously with the opposite sex

To SCRAT ABOUT - fuss aimlessly over small chores

SOME NOUNS:

BARM POTS, SWANK POTS, CRACK POTS, TOSS POTS - folk with varying characteristics

A COUGH DROP - a humorous person

PADDIWAK - nice mixture of mud and water

A SNIG - an eel

FOLLOW-ME-LADS - ...ribbons dangling from the back of a girl's hat

A SNECK - a door latch

DIALECT:

Dialect was frequently delivered by the mouthful, with no breathing breaks at all or with odd ones here and there at unnatural intervals. It was quite foreign to the Southerners! (Translations in brackets)

1. WEEZEGONNAGERRUSDINNAS (*We are going to get our dinners.)*

2. EESEZEEANTADDIT (*He says he has not had it.*)

3. ASTERSINIM? (*Have you seen him?*)

4. GERRITETTEN (*Get it eaten.*)

5. PURREMINEER (*Put them in here.*)

6. THALAVTERGURRUZANEWUN (*You will have to get us a new one.*)

7. LERIM PURRIZATON (*Let him put his hat on.*)

8. OOWUREEWEE WUREEWEEISEL? (*Who was he with, was he by himself?*)

9. DUSTER WANNAGOO OOAM? (*Do you want to go home?*)

10. EESEDEEDID BURRABETEEDIDNA (*He said he did, but I bet he didn't!*)

11. OWDOODICK OWSTERDOOIN? (*Hello Dick. How are you doing?*)

12. LERRUZ GERRUZ IMBUX (*Let us get our Hymn books.*)

13. YONLASSEL CUMTANUGUD! (*That girl will come to no good!*)

14. EEDURZNT PURRIZED INTWATTER (*He dare not put his head in the water.*)

15. LERRER GERRONTBIKE (*Let her get on the bike.*)

16. WILTER GEEUZ YONGRUTTATI? (*Will you give us that large potato.*)

17. SUMONUZ GORRAGERROFF (*Some of us will have to get off.*)

18. WEEZGORRA GERRUZANSWESHT (*We are going to get our hands washed.*)

19. ALTELTIM BUREEWUNTLISSEN (*I told him but he wouldn't listen.*)

20. EEZGONNA GERRA LORRABRASSFERIT (*He's going to get a lot of money for it.*)

1912

IT'S A BIG WORLD!

Children needed to be taught that, although they had never been out of Carnforth, there WAS a whole lot of Britain OUT THERE, and even foreign countries away across wide oceans - wider by far than the waters of Morecambe Bay. Geography lessons and talks about current events were necessary to expand young outlooks.

In January, children at the Church of England School were shown the globe and asked to point to the South Pole. They were disappointed to learn that the famous explorer, Captain Scott, had finally reached there only to discover that the Norwegian, Amundsen, had beaten him by a month.

HOME DISCIPLINE

Many fathers of large families in our community hung up one of their leather belts on the living-room wall. A parent simply pointing to it was usually a sufficient enough deterrent to discipline the children on most occasions.

Young ones were taught to obey their teachers, to respect the Police and cause them no trouble, to show due deference to the Clergy, and for boys to tip their caps politely to ladies and anyone in authority. "Manners maketh Man."

CRAFTY LADIES

Artistic housewives were still making useful umbrella stands from earthenware drainage pipes. Now, they were covering them with putty and pressing in broken pieces of pretty pottery. Although now in fragments, that floral teapot, which was once a wedding present from Auntie Fanny, could still be remembered with affection; that was much nicer than throwing it into the midden at the back of the earth closet in the backyard!

NO JOGGING

The usual exercise for Sunday afternoons was GOING FOR A WALK and taking a bunch of flowers to a family grave in Warton Churchyard. Armed with walking sticks, couples set off down Warton Road and made their way alongside the enormously high Iron Works wall to Millhead (its Sunday name. On weekdays it was usually called Dudley).

The gentlemen wore their best navy-blue serge suits, shirts with stiff, white celluloid collars and smart bowler hats. The ladies had on dark costumes with knee-length jackets, and around their necks were fox-furs, whose snarling jaws were firmly clamped on to their long bushy tails to hold them in position.

The ladies' wore wide-brimmed hats were lavishly decorated with flowers and feathers, and had to be anchored firmly to the hair with hat-pins, and veils which covered their faces and tied under their chins.

This was not comfortable attire for a 3-mile walk and there were hopes that, some day, Carnforth would have its own burial place.

COLD FACTS

There was a big freeze throughout the land in February, with temperatures dropping dangerously low. This gave cause for deep concern, because many miners were on strike. Whatever would Carnforth do if local coal supplies ran out?

Smoky, industrialised Carnforth viewed from Warton Crag. All houses had coal fires and the Railway, the Iron Works and the Gas Works all burned coal.

Every house had a coal fire in a big iron range, which not only heated the living-room but was the means of cooking meals, either in the fireside oven or in pans over the flames. Most ranges had a boiler at the side for heating water to wash pots ... and people. Scalding hot water had to be carried very carefully in 'lading' cans, and poured into a tin bowl in the shallow, brown back-kitchen slop-stone. A big iron kettle was usually 'singing' on the fire-side hob, ready for the making of a nice cup of tea or the filling of a stone hot-water bottle to warm the bed in the icy regions upstairs.

Without coal, life would come to a standstill. Already, one million workers were laid off because of the miners' strike. Carnforth was fortunate in having contact with any pits still working:

1. Along the canal from the South Lancashire Coalfield.

2. The Furness Railway to the Cumberland mines.

3. The Midland line to the Yorkshire Coalfield.

It was a great relief to the whole country when, to settle the dispute, the Government brought in The Coal Miners' Bill, which established for the first time the principle of a minimum wage. The Union of Mineworkers had asked for at least 5s (25p) a day for men and 2s (10p) for boys.

VANDALS

Militant suffragettes, still demanding VOTES FOR WOMEN, caused thousands of £s damage in a window-smashing rampage throughout the London's West End. They had stones and hammers

HIDDEN IN THEIR MUFFS, and even hurled missiles at Number 10, Downing Street. More than 120 were arrested, among them their leader Emmeline Pankhurst.

"Unladylike behaviour like that gets NO support from us!" decided Carnforth Grandmas, as they donned their bonnets, furs and muffs before setting out for church.

OUCH!

Having a minor operation or having a tooth extracted could be a very painful experience in our town (or any other!). Our Dr Jackson was registered as a surgeon, so presumably was permitted to administer some anaesthetic on a pad over the patients faces - cocaine, chloroform, or ether. Now, an American surgeon was condemning all three as unnecessary, dangerously addictive and likely to produce a race of fiends!

[Oh dear!]

It was recommended that they should be replaced by nitrous oxide, which gives no unpleasant after-effects and is not poisonous. A prize was offered for the design of a machine to deliver the gas.

DISASTER AT SEA

There was great sadness on April 23rd when news arrived that THE TITANIC, pride of the White Star Line, had sunk on her Maiden Voyage from Southampton to America. The great liner, proclaimed as unsinkable, had gone down within hours of striking an iceberg and more than 1,500 of the 2,340 passengers and crew had drowned. With all her lights still shining and the band bravely playing, she had nose-dived into the icy depths.

There was much conjecture around Carnforth:

1. Had the gigantic liner been speeding through the dangerous ice-field in an attempt to win the Blue Riband award?

2. Had there been a shortage of lifeboats?

3. Had the crew been partying and failed to keep a sharp lookout?

Local interest was increased when it was rumoured that the conductor of the band, which was playing 'Nearer My God To Thee' as the ship plunged into the sea, was a man from Barrow. Sympathetic eyes scanned the Bay to where Barrow's huge cranes were silhouetted against the skyline.

SADNESS IN PRESTON STREET

Carnforth's Salvationists were sad to learn of the death of their General, William Booth, on Aug 20th. He had started to preach when he was 17, and was expelled from 2 Methodist Churches because he wished to preach in the streets rather than in pulpits.

The Salvation Army had adopted its name and

uniform in 1877. Now, not including Carnforth, there 3,999 corps and 12,999 officers.

RAIN

In August, England had the heaviest rainfall on record. In some areas, 6 inches fell in 12 hours. There were widespread floods, especially in the Fen District, and Norwich, along with some other towns, was completely cut off.

As usual, Carnforth had more than its fair share and umbrellas were in frequent use. When the coastline across the Bay was very clearly visible, that forecast RAIN. When it was not visible at all, that meant it was ALREADY raining.

DEFENCE

At Carnforth's Men's Societies, worries were expressed about our country's defences.

During the summer, the Admiralty recalled some warships from Malta and transferred them to the North Sea. The German Fleet was growing and Britain was crippled by strikes - the dockers this time. Winston Churchill, First Lord of the Admiralty, was anxious and wanted to expand the naval budget so that a large shipbuilding programme could be speeded up. 4 dreadnoughts, 8 cruisers, 20 destroyers and some submarines were planned to be built.

Vickers machine-guns, deadly weapons with terrific killing power, were being introduced into the Army to strengthen our land forces, whilst to defend us in the air the Royal Flying Corps was set up.

Surely it was not contemplated that Germany might start a war with us?

Our King George and their Kaiser Wilhelm II were such friendly cousins!

MORPHY'S MILL

Since Ramsay's Sewing Mill had been bought by Morphys, extensions and innovations had taken place and there were now 140 employees, mostly girls.

The Mill Girls in their Sunday Best and all wearing big hats, on a company outing, probably to the grounds of Morphy's house near Holme. Hired waggonettes would take them there.

During the summer, a large party was taken on a day trip and photographed in the grounds of a big house. *[Perhaps it was their employer's home, situated between Milnthorpe and Holme].*

It is quite unlikely that any 'shinanicking' went on during the outing, considering that the proportion of women to men was In the ratio of 35 females to 1 male. In addition, it would have been difficult for the girls to behave with anything less than decorum, as they were wearing ankle-length dresses and balancing on their heads enormously wide-brimmed hats, heavily-decorated with a wealth of fruit and flowers.

Transporting large groups of people presented difficulties unless their destination was within walking distance of a railway station. *[It could be that horse-drawn coaches or wagonettes were hired from 'The Station Hotel', or maybe 'The Queen's', for this mill outing.]*

THAT TUNE!

The favourite song being whistled around our streets was, "IT'S A LONG WAY TO TIPPERARY".

[A few years later, this tune was to have some very sad connections!]

1913

SHOPPING AROUND

1. THE CARNFORTH REMINDER was printed, published and distributed free by W J WEEKS, Printer and Bill Poster, Telephone 11.

2,000 copies were required to cover the district, and people found the advertisements by local tradesmen and the railway timetables very informative and useful.

On the L.N.W.R. Line, a train leaving here at 12.12pm arrived in London at 5.40pm. The 1.25pm train from Carnforth arrived in Whitehaven at 4.45 on the Furness Line, and on the Midland Line the 10.12 train from here reached Leeds at 12.52pm.

2. THE CARNFORTH 1d and 6½d BAZAAR, at the top of Market Street, proudly announced, "NO VALUE LIKE OURS!" All our 6½d goods are the best value the world can produce, and plenty to choose from! House-hold Goods, Toys and Useful Presents. Come and see our PENNY GOODS - the largest variety in the district."

3. MISS WOOLSTENCROFT, HALL GOWAN COTTAGE, was a highly qualified TEACHER OF MUSIC AND ART, and gave piano, harmony, theory, painting and drawing lessons, either at her home or at that of any pupil.

4. J SHARP, 40 Market Street, HOSIER AND

DRAPER, sold Seasonable Underwear at his shop, 'THE SIGN OF THE STOCKING.'

5. J & L GERRARD, 5 Market Street, advertised themselves as the oldest established complete house-furnishers & cabinet-makers in the district (est. 1875).

They had a selection of linoleums, oilcloths, carpets, bedsteads, bedding, tea, dinner and chamber services, bassinets and pushchairs. A Harvey vacuum cleaner cost £3 10s, but could be hired for 2s 6d (12½p) per day.

[If this was an electrically-powered machine, no working-class people here would be able to plug it in. No electricity!]

6. W J WEEKS sold H K SMOKING MIXTURE at 4½d (2p) per ounce - ideal tobacco for smokers (or chewers!)

7. FREDERICK MOON, Ladies' and Gentlemen's Tailor, 48 Market Street, invited customers to try his 2 guineas suits (£2 2s)

8. JOHN MURRAY (Drapery, Hosiery, Child's-wear) said, "Our blouses, at 1s 11½d (10p), defy competition." And added, "Stockings knitted to order". His shop was at 2 Stanley Street.

9. ROWLINSON & EDMONSON were House Painters at 23 King Street or Cragbank. (Throughout Britain 10,000 painters and decorators were on strike for better pay)

[These tradesmen, like in all our town, were working for themselves and so were anxious to, "get stuck in and see the job finished well".]

10. J E NICHOLSON, Dispensing Chemist, 42 Market Street, had wise advice for housewives preparing to attack on the SPRING CLEANING front: "Remember MORSE'S DISTEMPER - unequalled, easy to apply, durable, ARTISTIC(?) and does NOT rub."

11. "EGGS AT 2d each," promised DOCKRAY'S. "To have hens laying through the cold, wet weather, use BISCUIT MEAL or BISCUIT DUST - 10s 6d (52p) per hundred-weight. Much better than Indian meal."

12. F POSTLETHWAITE, Chimney Sweep, had a painted advertisement on the gable-end of his home, 1 ALEXANDRA ROAD. (Some daring householders, with heads for heights, had a go at sweeping their own chimneys by lowering a bunch of prickly holly down the flue from the roof. Mr Postlethwaite was also a window-cleaner but again, that was a job folks could do themselves in order to save expense.)

13. CARNFORTH LENDING LIBRARY. At the newsagent's shop, 38 Market Street, SIX NEW BOOKS had been recently added and their titles listed.

[Carnforthians must have been waiting with baited breath for such an exciting event.]

14. BATTERSBY'S had a building alongside Lancaster Road, near the junction with Haws Hill *[demolished a few years ago].*

They advertised themselves as CARNFORTH CARRIERS and hired out flat carts pulled by horses.

CARS AHEAD

W LAWRENCE established premises adjoining the AUCTION MART (off Market Street, behind the Queen's Hotel). He advertised himself as a MOTOR BODY BUILDER - car repairs, windscreens, cape-hoods, painting, varnishing etc.

Carnforth was way behind the times, however, in the world of motors. In March, the first MORRIS OXFORD car left the factory, built by William Morris at Cowley, near Oxford, whilst in America motor-production was speeding ahead.

Since 1908, Henry Ford's factory had operated a stationary assembly line using mass-produced precision parts. In October, he unveiled a 250ft long MOVING assembly line, at which each worker performed one specialised function as the vehicle under assembly passed him. This reduced the labour required to assemble a chassis to under 2 man hours, and Ford hoped to manufacture 250,000 Model Ts next year.

Just thinking about that, at his newly established premises in Carnforth, made W Lawrence feel very dizzy!

A SITE TO WATCH

When his wife died, Mr Tom Metcalfe and his 5 children lived for a while in a tent pitched in a field belonging to his parent's farm. Probably, at the time, there was insufficient room to accommodate them at the farmhouse which, with a nearby barn, stood alongside LOWER NORTH ROAD.

Camping on the site of Carnforth Council School. Widower Tom Metcalfe and his five children in the field near his parent's farm.

The field and an orchard behind the farm were being considered as part of a site where a big, new school might be built.

[The farm, built in 1688, is Carnforth's 2nd oldest house. The oldest is HAGG FARM, near the River Keer, off Shore Road, which is dated 1638.]

TALKING ABOUT TENTS

In a snow-covered tent in the wastes of America, a relief party found the frozen bodies of Captain Scott and his companions. A diary, left by Scott, confirmed the deaths of 2 more explorers: Petty Officer Evans and Captain Oates - the latter bravely walking from the tent into the blizzard, sacrificing his life because he knew the others would have a better chance of journeying to safety without him.

HOLY TENTS

On some memorable occasions, very large tents were pitched on available spare land in Carnforth, e.g. THE MARKET GROUND, the field in front of HIGHFIELD TERRACE or the flat ground near THE CANAL COTTAGES.

The visitors were teams of Evangelists, whose mission was to save our inhabitants from eternal damnation. Those HOT GOSPELLERS preached that, unless people turned from sin, repented and were SAVED, they would eventually be cast into the fiery furnace of HELL. Not everyone agreed with their form of evangelism, and a tale was told of one sceptical individual who asked the preacher, "If I'm saved and become an angel, how will I manage to get my shirt over my wings?"

The sharp reply to that query was said to have been, "That will not be one of your worries, my dear man. Your problem will be how you will pull up your trousers over your long, forked tail!"

Those visiting preachers were often young handsome men with charming personalities, and crowds flocked to the tents to hear a different form of religion from that to which they were accustomed.

Some people were so impressed with a BOY PREACHER that they treasured his photograph for many years. His angelic features, framed in long wavy hair, proved attractive to all females, young and old! It is thought that his Christian name was Laurie and that he was an American.

A SAD END

News of this death was not received with sadness by all the people of Carnforth. Some, mostly men, were heard to say, "Serve her right!" One of those troublesome suffragettes had been killed at the Derby when she ran on the course, amongst the galloping race-horses, and tried to stop the one which was owned by the king.

There was a vast procession of suffragettes at her funeral and 4 of them, dressed in white with black sashes, flanked the coffin as it was carried on an open carriage, drawn by 4 black horses. Heading the procession were dozens of clergy and 10 bands played mournful funeral music. Behind the coffin were 4 vehicles, laden with hundreds of wreaths from all over the world.

Carnforth funerals left our churches and then set off on the long, slow journey to Warton Churchyard. Glass-sided hearses, drawn by black horses wearing nodding black plumes, would be hired from the Station Hotel or The Queen's. If they could be afforded, funeral coaches would also be hired. If not, all the mourners walked in a sad cortege behind the hearse. All pedestrians along the route stood with heads reverently bowed, men having removed their hats.

IN LOVING MEMORY

Dying was a serious business! In preparation for it, folk with "not two 'a' pennies (½d) to rub together" regularly paid out a few coppers in INSURANCE MONEY to ensure that, when their time came, they could have a proper send-off. One drawer in the bedroom dressing table was reserved for 'laying-out' garments, including long, white, hand-knitted stockings, a white night-shirt and a beautiful white nightgown, carefully tucked and trimmed with hand-crocheted lace.

Most streets had a woman who attended to the neighbours as they came into, or departed from, this Life. She was the local midwife and could also be called upon to lay out the dead.

After a funeral, families wore black for a set period of mourning. Those who could not afford to do so wore a black arm-band as a sign of respect.

Funeral cards were printed, and dispatched in black-edged envelopes. Handkerchiefs, too, had black borders, and even special mourning jewellery was worn, e.g. brooches made of jet.

A Carnforthian's EXIT was given almost as much attention as a Pharaoh's entry into his Pyramid.

FLYING BUSES

An express train, thundering through Carnforth station amidst clouds of smoke and steam, was an awesome sight to witness, and people felt that our town was an important link in the chain of transport development. There were folk in some remote rural areas who had never seen a train!

In October, when newspapers gave reports on an air display at Hendon, it had to be admitted that even Carnforth was falling behind the times. An aero-bus had set up a record by carrying aloft 10 people, including the pilot. A BUS WITH WINGS! And we hadn't even a 4-wheeled, terrestrial one serving our town!

UNSEEMLY BEHAVIOUR

Kaiser Wilhelm II issued an order to the men of the German army and navy requesting them not to dance either the tango or the two-step, and to avoid families who did.

Failure to observe the 'REQUEST' would result in dismissal. The American authorities would not tolerate any "funny business" in public either. In New York, a couple was arrested for kissing in the street on Christmas Day.

Even in England, the behaviour of some people needed to be kept under control. During the summer, a woman in Richmond was seized for wearing a SPLIT SKIRT - the hussy! Of course, no ladies in Carnforth would commit such indiscretions.

IN SERVICE

About this time, Annie Barnham left the work she loved at Morphy's Mill and went into service as a maid at the home of Mr and Mrs Thomas Faithwaite Jackson, a childless couple who lived at Meresbeck, up North Road. Maybe the change-over was organised by Mrs Taylor of 16 Kellet Road, who ran a SERVANT'S REGISTRY. Annie made the move because the family of her fiancé, Thomas Wilkinson, was of the opinion that being in service was better than doing demeaning work in a mill. The Wilkinsons had firm religious beliefs and came of good Lancashire stock with an agricultural background. Christianity teaches the value of service. Jesus said, "I came not to RULE but to SERVE", and knelt to wash His Disciples' feet.

In Victorian Society, the term GOING INTO SERVICE was regarded as a kind of trade or profession. Young people went to live-in at a big house and were trained to be footmen, gardeners, butlers, cooks, maids, etc. In an ideal situation, they served their masters faithfully and, in return, were taken care of physically and spiritually. Being in service was a position of honour.

The idea had originated way back in time during THE AGE OF CHIVALRY, when, at the age of 7, a boy could go and live in the castle of a noble knight and became a PAGE. To him, it was a duty and a privilege to wait on his Lord at table and serve him food and wine. He was taught to love Peace and Justice, and to treat ladies with respect. When he was 14, he learnt to ride and use arms as instructed by a squire and, by the time he was 21, he was considered to have served his apprenticeship and might become a Squire or a Knight himself.

For many years, young Carnforthians had chosen to go into service when leaving school, because there was little alternative employment before the railways and the Iron Works offered work for males and the Sewing Mill for females.

There were members of some very large families who still chose to leave a crowded home and take up a live-in job at a nearby farm or large house. Ideally, that could be good, but sadly there were mean, harsh masters and mistresses who could make an employee's life one of deprivation and drudgery.

A MEDICAL REPORT

With a population of just over 3000, all Carnforth's families knew each other fairly well. RESPECTABILITY was the key word in their lives, and each street and terrace set its own standards. However poor they were, families strove to pay their way, keep clean and feed their children as well as possible.

Fortunately, basic foods such as bread, margarine, milk, jam, corned beef etc. were quite cheap, and the wolf was kept away from the doors of Russell Road, Preston Street, Haws Hill, Edward Street etc.

Reading the report of the Chief Schools' Medical Officer in the newspapers set Carnforth tongues tut-tutting. He stated that, of the country's 6 million children, about one third were unhygienically dirty, had eye defects, hearing troubles, inflamed tonsils, ringworm and serious illnesses such as tuberculosis.

"Why were some parents so shiftless?" our townsfolk wondered.

RELIGION

Carnforth was a town full of fervent believers, and on Sundays all our churches were full. Each had its own group of faithful followers, who worked hard to raise money for church expenses and enjoyed a full social life together. There was no animosity between the different faiths.

Roman Catholics still did not have a church here, so they walked along the canal banks or on the main road to worship at St Mary of the Angels at Bolton-le-Sands. When their children were 7 years old, they were considered old enough to walk to the school there. Until then, they attended one of the

Carnforth schools and were allowed to withdraw from Prayers and Scripture lessons if their parents so wished.

No one made an issue of that, and Protestant and Roman Catholic children played happily together. The grown-ups joined in all the town's activities and marched peacefully side-by-side in any celebratory processions.

FAVOURITE SONG OF 1913

The best selling sheet music of the year was, "HELLO! HELLO! WHO'S YOUR LADY FRIEND?" If you lived in Carnforth it had better be your very OWN wife or sweetheart ... OR ELSE!

1914

THE NEW SCHOOL

The British School was closed and the pupils and staff were transferred to the newly-built school in LOWER NORTH ROAD, on the site which had been the orchard of the Metcalfes' Farm.

Every morning, straight after PRAYER TIME at the former National School on Lancaster Road, pupils were fed a daily dose of SCRIPTURE, when they were taught not only stories from the Bible but also the beliefs of the Church of England. The vicar called in at regular intervals to make sure that the scholars could chant the CREED and the CATECHISM.

Looking up Oliver Street from Hawk Street. The British School at the top. Sunday Services were held there until The Emmanuel Congregational Church was opened in 1897.

Many non-conformists in the town were not happy with such indoctrination, and that is why, in 1880, people of the Emmanuel Congregational faith had built a CHAPEL-SCHOOL before they had a church of their own. The Headmaster, Mr R T Barnard, had been appointed in 1897 and at one time his monthly wage had been £4, his assistant's 10s 0d and a monitor 8s 0d - all paid by the Congregational minister, the Reverend Towers.

The move to the smart, modern COUNCIL SCHOOL, with its many facilities, caused rejoicing amongst the non-conformists of our town, and some 'C of E' parents risked the displeasure of their vicar by also transferring their children to the NEW SCHOOL (at it became known).

The Bell-cote which topped the old school and now stands by the doorway of the C of E school. The bell is said to be in the cellar of the church.

WISE ADVICE IN THE CARNFORTH REMINDER

To preserve your health and keep you fit by destroying ALL infectious germs, use HOYLE'S PURE CARBOLIC SOAP. ("Reet powerful stuff were that!")

A GLOW IN THE NIGHT

Bedrooms could be dark, frightening places for children. Oil-lamps were far too dangerous to stand near beds, and a candle in a holder, which had been used to light the way upstairs, had to be extinguished when the children were tucked-up in bed. With heads snuggled on a feather pillow with a long bolster under it, they were covered with a sheet, blankets and a pretty patch-work quilt – all highly inflammable.

Caring parents, who understood their young ones' fear of the dark, went to the big Co-op Grocery shop in New Street and bought some PRICE'S NIGHT LIGHTS, which were stood in a saucer containing a little water before being lit. They would give a comforting glow for up to 10 hours, and were reassuringly described as, "THE BURGLAR'S HORROR".

Burglars in Carnforth? What a ridiculous idea. Doors didn't even need to be locked and could stay wide open all day in good weather. The night lights were effective in that they prevented BOGEY-MEN from lurking in dark corners.

A GOOD WORKMAN

Joseph Walmesley, Painter and Decorator of Scotland Road, guaranteed that he would do a good job ... and he did!

The Congregational Church (opened in 1897) needed decorating. Here is the bill for Joseph's work:

Distempering, painting & decorating inside church - £25 14s 3d

Painting & re-gilding of light pendants - £2 0s 0d

Making good & distempering ceiling - 5s 9d

Total £28 0s 0d

Painting exterior of church:

1. Preparing all wood and ironwork

2. Burning off old paint

3. Repainting 2 or 3 coats. Varnishing.

Total £6 15s 7d

SOUVENIR OF WESLEY CHURCH

Bazaar May 20th, 21st & 22nd

"Quotations and Recipes" - *Printed by J. W. Smith, Market Street*

A CURE FOR LONELINESS

Best cure: get outside yourself and do something for somebody.

Human Nature is the same as Garden Nature. If you leave flowers on plants they will cease to bloom, e.g. if you do not cut sweet peas every day, they will not last a month.

So, if you do not give out your small happiness to others, it will soon wither and cease to sweeten your life.

A CURE FOR COMMON DISORDER OF THE MOUTH

1oz of Good Nature

1oz of herb called MIND YOUR OWN BUSINESS.

Mix these with a little charity and understanding, 2-3 sprigs of Keep Your Tongue Between Your Teeth.

Simmer the whole in a vessel of Circumspection for a short time and it will be ready for use.

When you feel a violent itching in the mouth and tongue, take 1 teaspoon of the above and hold it closely in your mouth till the symptoms pass away.

THINK ON THESE THINGS:

1. Even an umbrella has its ups and downs

2. It's not the man who has the most
   Who gives the most away,
   Nor is it he who knows the most
   Who has the most to say.

THAT NEW SCHOOL

Bertha Barnham, aged 12, was amongst the first group of senior girls to go from THE CHURCH OF ENGLAND SCHOOL to the COOKERY AND WOODWORK CENTRE, which had been built in front of the new COUNCIL SCHOOL on Lower North Road.

Girls and boys over the age of 11 from the schools of nearby villages also went to the Centre for practical lessons and, because there were no buses, the pupils had to walk. Boys were taught to do manly jobs, whilst girls learnt how to do women's tasks. *[Extremely sexist!]*

Through the entrance marked BOYS and up the stairs went the young males, and in the classroom there, they learnt how to use hammer and nails, and produced wobbly pan-stands and pipe-racks.

Females went through the GIRLS' doorway and commenced LAUNDRY LESSONS, by learning how to wash handkerchiefs. *[Ha! Ha! Teach your granddaughter how to suck eggs!]*

Those girls who were at the older end of a big family could already tackle a big washday when their mothers were 'off-colour'.

In COOKERY LESSONS, they were instructed in the art of making Rock Cakes and Spotted Dick, but most of them could have provided a good meal for the family more efficiently than the teacher!

LIGHTEN OUR DARNKESS

The large oil-lamp, which stood in the centre of the table in most Carnforth living-rooms, needed lots of attention. Paraffin had to be brought in a can from the Co-op Furnishing and Hardware Department, in Market Street, when the level in the lamp's glass bowl was seen to be getting low. New wicks could be bought there too and they needed to be kept trimmed so that the flame burnt evenly. The tall lamp-glass had to be handled very carefully when smoke-marks were being cleaned from its interior with newspaper. "Mind that lamp!" children were constantly being told.

In February, eyebrows were raised in amazement when newspaper reports stated, "Marconi has announced that he can light a lamp 6 miles away by wireless power."

A chap in Lancaster lighting a lamp in Russell Road? Whatever next?

STRIKES

A lot of arguments went on at the Midland Shed (off Scotland Road). Two million workers were on strike in Britain: electricians, dockers, building workers and now railwaymen in some areas.

Would our countrymen never pull together?

That German Kaiser had recently launched the world's biggest ship: THE BISMARK. Those Huns were up to something!

THOSE FEROCIOUS FEMALES . . . AGAIN

Our townspeople were quite distressed when they read, in April, that suffragettes had destroyed Yarmouth Pier by fire. What if activists burnt the pier at Morecambe?

Carnforth folk loved to join other holiday-makers and stroll along it on sunny days, with gentle waves lapping below. It felt like being on a luxury cruise-liner in the Mediterranean Sea. And that magnificent building at the end of the pier? Like an Indian palace! That was Morecambe's answer to the Taj Mahal.

Morecambe's magnificent Central Pier.

Our townspeople were quite distressed when they read, in April, that suffragettes had destroyed Yarmouth Pier by fire. What if activists burnt the pier at Morecambe? Carnforth folk loved to join other holiday-makers and stroll along it on sunny days, with gentle waves lapping below. It felt like being on a luxury cruise-liner in the Mediterranean Sea. And that magnificent building at the end of the pier? Like an Indian palace! That was Morecambe's answer to the Taj Mahal.

Those troublesome suffragettes boasted that they were waging all-out guerrilla warfare in their fight to win VOTES FOR WOMEN. Recently, they had raided the British Museum and Regent's Park, and bombed St Paul's Cathedral, the homes of several Government ministers and some Scottish churches. They had wrecked the golf-villa belonging to Lloyd George, committed arson attacks at Kew Gardens and posted many letter bombs.

If only their hatred could have been directed against Germany, they could have knocked Kaiser Wilhelm II off his perch and have sorted out the German nation once and for all!

DARK DAYS AHEAD!

On June 28th, a 19-year-old student shot and killed Archduke Franz Ferdinand, heir to the Austro-Hungarian throne, at SARAJEVO, capital of BOSNIA. He said afterwards that he wanted to take revenge for the oppression of the Serbian people whose capital was BELGRADE.

A tidal wave of horror and indignation swept over Europe in the wake of the atrocity, but Carnforth folk were not very concerned because those far-away places had unfamiliar names, and foreign countries were forever “fratching”.

A writer in the Daily Chronicle wrote of the terrible event as A CLAP OF THUNDER OVER EUROPE. Sadly, it was thunder that eventually led to a horrendous storm and, before long, our town was engulfed along with the rest of the continent, as those mighty powers Germany and Russia took opposite sides.

When Britain declared war on Germany on August 4th, the news was greeted by cheering crowds in London and, along with thousands of others, some patriotic and adventurous young Carnforth men rushed to enlist. They were desperate to get overseas to the fields of war in Europe, because they thought the conflict might be over before Christmas. On Aug 19th, a BRITISH EXPEDITIONARY FORCE of 700,000 men landed in France, most of them with little or no knowledge of warfare.

CARNFORTH'S GERMAN

A great wave of anti-German feeling swept over Britain - even inoffensive German ‘Sausage’ dogs were given hefty kicks, just because they were not good, patriotic English bulldogs! There was a major round-up of aliens throughout the land, and wholesale arrests on espionage charges. Soon, 300 suspected spies were detained, and the Olympic Complex in London became a CONCENTRATION CAMP.

Carnforth people were on the alert for dubious characters, and who sounded the most suspicious to them? MRS GERMAN, of course, who had a tripe and fish and chip shop in Victoria Buildings (lower New Street, opposite to the side of the Station Hotel).

Down went her trade like a stone thrown into the canal! Accusing eyes followed her every move. Was she walking down to Shore Lane and flashing signals with her torch to U-boats, which might be lurking in the bay, or waving to a Zeppelin when she walked up North Road, pretending to exercise her dog?

Upset by the animosity surrounding her, she tried spelling and pronouncing that despicable surname in a different way. G-E-R-M-A-I-N-E - Germaine. All in vain! She was still classed as a German enemy, and some bigoted folk would have liked to put her aboard a ship in Heysham Harbour and deport her to the Isle of Man to join other Germans in the concentration camps there.

Poor, innocent woman! She had pure English blood in her veins, which was more could be said for our Royal Family! Prince Louis of Battenberg was made to resign at Britain's First Sea Lord. His family later Anglicised their name to Mountbatten, and King George decided to drop the names of various

Germanic states and to adopt WINDSOR as The Royal Family's surname from now on.

VOLUNTEERS WANTED

On billboards all around our town appeared huge posters of the head and shoulders of Lord Kitchener, with a finger pointing directly at each man in Carnforth and the message, "BRITAIN, our country, wants YOU".

JOIN OUR ARMY.

"God Save The King".

The Prime Minister, Herbert Asquith, called for 500,000 men to sign up for the army, because the Government wanted to put 1,200,000 men in the field as quickly as possible.

Quite a number of young men in Carnforth answered the call and joined the Army, and a few became sailors. None became Airmen.

Aeroplanes were changing the grim face of War, and the enemies were flying over each other's lines on reconnaissance surveys. Britain had lost its first plane to enemy ground-fire, and one-of-ours had shot down one-of-theirs by machine gun fire, just as it was about to drop a handmade bomb. Some planes threw out hundreds of flechettes (like steel darts) to cause casualties.

THE WAR ESCALATED

Carnforth praised God that it was on the west coast of England. Towns on the shores of the North Sea were in grave danger. Three German warships shelled Scarborough, Whitby and Hartlepool.

News from the front was very depressing. A trench barrier stretched from the Swiss border to the North Sea and there was stalemate as the Allies and the Germans faced each other with a NO-MAN'S-LAND of barbed wire and mud between the trenches.

Carnforth 'Tommies' wrote home about the British Front in Flanders, where the town of YPRES was known to them as 'WIPERS'. (At that town alone there had been 100,000 British casualties.) Anxious wives, parents and sweethearts were comforted to know that their dear ones were still alive. Especially treasured were postcards depicting flowers, birds, butterflies and the flags of the Allies, all beautifully embroidered in coloured silks, as were the messages, "SOUVENIR FROM FRANCE", "FOR FREEDOM", "UNITED FOR LIBERTY" & "GREETINGS FROM THE TRENCHES".

On the back of one such card, sent to his WIFE, a solider had written:

Dear Hilda,

Sorry, but there is a tiny card inside marked "TO MY SISTER". I never noticed it before, but never mind. It will do, won't it?

BONSOIR, MA CHERIE.

Hilda didn't mind the little card slotted under the embroidered flowers, but why ever had her dear husband signed off with those mysterious words "Bonsoir, ma Cherie". She did so hope there was nothing sinister about them.

THE FIRST WARTIME CHRISTMAS

War came to a brief halt on Dec 25th, the day of Christ's birth. Both British and German troops emerged from their trenches in one corner of the Western Front. They waved to each other and tried to communicate. German cigars were exchanged for English jam (some perhaps made from the blackberries picked from hedgerows up Carnforth's Walker Lane?). It was reported that some soldiers even enjoyed a friendly game of football with the enemy, before both sides returned to their trenches and made ready to start shooting each other again next morning. *[Oh! The madness and sadness of War!]*

At home, here in Carnforth, people sang, "KEEP THE HOME FIRES BURNING", for that is what they were doing whilst their loved ones were far away on foreign battlefields.

Our town was firm in its Christian Faith and, at the end of this first year of World War I, many were the prayers offered up to God, beseeching Him to bring PEACE ON EARTH and to keep their men safe.

This seems to be an appropriate time at which to bring to an end this little tale of how Carnforth coped with the rapidly changing times of the early 20th century. It was the age when my parents grew up, became sweethearts and eventually were married at the Parish Church. Many were the stories they told me about life in Carnforth in those distant days.

New ideas, inventions and innovations took quite a time to reach this north-western corner of Lancashire from the big cities, but they did arrive eventually. There had been 3 monarchs on the throne - Victoria, Edward VII and George V - and life in Carnforth had change considerably since Victorian times.

I was born in 1915, and this story is concluded in the final book in the series: *A Childhood in Carnforth*.

In the true style of our home town, for the time being, I'll say some fond farewells:

"TA RA!"

"TOODLE-OO"

"SITHEE!"

REFERENCES

The Mannex Directory of Lancaster & 16 miles Around, 1911.

Guide to Carnforth & District, Published in 1908.

The Census Forms of 1901 and 1911.

Extracts from *THE LANCASTER GUARDIAN,* by kind permission of the present editor.

Extracts from *THE CHRONICLE OF THE 20th CENTURY.*

Old Lakeland Transport, by Irvine Hunt.

Looking at History, R J Unstead.

Extracts from *Carnforth's Monthly Reminder of 1913.*

The Guinness Book of Names.

If you have enjoyed this book, please consider reviewing it on Amazon or Goodreads (or both).

And feel free visit the Lundarien Press website for more titles by Marion Russell and other authors:

www.lundarienpress.com

Made in the USA
Columbia, SC
21 April 2017